FROM REBELLION TO RESTORATION

Arnold Valentin Wallenkampf

REVIEW AND HERALD® PUBLISHING ASSOCIATION
WASHINGTON, DC 20039-0555
HAGERSTOWN, MD 21740

This book was
Edited by James Cavil
Designed by Bill Kirstein
Cover photo by M. Thonig/H. Armstrong Roberts/
inset: Robert Ayres
Type set: 11/12 ZAPF

PRINTED IN U.S.A.

95 94 93 92 91 90   10 9 8 7 6 5 4 3 2 1

Library of Congress Cataloging-in-Publication Data
Wallenkampf, Arnold Valentin, 1913-
   From rebellion to restoration / Arnold Valentin Wallenkampf.
      p.   cm.
   Includes index.
   1. Bible.   O.T.   Ezekiel—Criticism, interpretation, etc.
I. Title.
BS1545.2.W34   1990
224'.406—dc20
                                                    90-47209
                                                    CIP

ISBN 0-8280-0614-8

Contents

Preface

The book of Ezekiel—the fourth-longest book in the Bible, after Psalms, Jeremiah, and Genesis—is probably one of the most neglected books in the entire Bible. Only some of the minor prophets equal or approach it in unfamiliarity, even among readers who are usually well acquainted with the Sacred Scriptures. The parts of Ezekiel probably best known are chapter 37, about the valley of dry bones; chapters 1 and 10, about the wheels; and possibly chapters 38 and 39, often thought of as speaking about Russia. And the familiarity with even the first three chapters mentioned may possibly rest only on the picturesque presentation of the contents of these chapters in Negro spirituals.

Ezekiel was a spokesman for God to the Jewish captives on the banks of the river Chebar in ancient Babylon during the first part of the sixth century B.C. He paints a picture of God embracing both His kindness and severity, referred to by Paul in Romans 11:22. But he reverses Paul's order. Ezekiel first shows the severity of God manifested in judgments on Israel and the surrounding nations in chapters 1-32.

The first 24 chapters of Ezekiel present the unhappy picture of doom and judgment on the kingdom of Judah because of her sins. This section ends with the beginning of Nebuchadnezzar's final siege of Jerusalem and the death of Ezekiel's wife. The death of Ezekiel's wife, the delight of the prophet's eyes, in a sense was a symbol of the destruction of Jerusalem, the pride and glory of the Jews. And so these met their end at the same time.

Section two of Ezekiel (chapters 25-32) contains judgments on and destruction of the surrounding nations. The doom of Judah is now in the past. Judgment falls now on some of those nations that have afflicted her.

The final section of the book (chapters 33-48) presents a different picture altogether. These chapters portray God's mercy and kindness. They breathe an atmosphere of hope and renewal with unlimited possibilities for restored Israel. In this section of Ezekiel, reunited Israel, comprising remnants of both former Israel and Judah, lives in security and peace in its ancestral land under the blessing of the new covenant experience presented in chapter 36. This experience is to be constantly sustained by the vivifying power of the Holy Spirit (see chapter 37).

The very finale of this section (chapters 38-48) is a rhapsody of blessings that will accrue to postexilic, born-again, and Spirit-directed Israel. Ezekiel pictures the peace and security restored Israel will enjoy under a renewed covenant relationship with God.

More than a half century later, after the release of all the captives in the East, the prophet Zechariah, in Jerusalem with the returned exiles, often echoes Ezekiel about Israel's glorious future. Ezekiel painted his stimulating picture for the encouragement of the captives lest they succumb to despair in what seemed to them hopeless captivity.

Zechariah gave his prophecies to bolster the flagging courage of the returned exiles as they tried to rebuild Jerusalem amid trials and difficulty.

This book, *From Rebellion to Restoration*, makes no attempt to discuss every chapter of the book of Ezekiel, but it does seek to illuminate some themes from the book that are important to Christians today.

Dr. Karl Barth mentioned that Calvin's commentary on Romans made the walls separating the sixteenth century from the first transparent! "Paul speaks," he said, "and the man of the sixteenth century hears" (in F. F. Bruce, *Commentary on the Book of the Acts* [Grand Rapids: Eerdmans Pub. Co., 1973], p. 9).

Fortunate is the writer who achieves that desirable goal. May the reader of this book hear God speak to him through His prophet Ezekiel as He guides His ancient people through dark storms and lingering shadows to the radiant sunshine of His constant love and care.

CHAPTER 1

TRIPLE
TRAGEDY

Based on Ezekiel 1:1-3; 2:1-5; 3:15; 24:16

Ezekiel received his prophetic call in his thirtieth year, the age at which an Israelite priest began his priestly ministry (see Num. 4:1-4).[1] He equated his own thirtieth year with "the fifth year of king Jehoiachin's captivity" (Eze. 1:2, KJV). This places his call at 592 B.C. According to this chronology Ezekiel was born in 622 B.C., during the reign of good king Josiah of Judah (640-609 B.C.). In keeping with the dates Ezekiel affixed to his prophecies, his prophetic ministry stretched from 592 B.C. about 22 years into the future.

Josiah became king at the age of 8 upon the assassination of his 24-year-old father. He was born and reared as a small boy in the very perverse and wicked environment of his grandfather Manasseh and father Amon. Even so, he resisted every temptation to walk in his father's and grandfather's footsteps.

With few counselors to encourage him in the right way, Josiah was nevertheless true to the God of Israel. Against the pattern of his day and surroundings "he began to seek the God of David his [long-ago dead paternal] father" (2 Chron. 34:3).

In the twelfth year of his reign Josiah began to clean out the idols and destroy the places of idol worship in Jerusalem and throughout his country (see verses 3-7). At the time

7

Ezekiel was born in 622, Josiah accentuated his reformation by repairing the Temple. During this repair Hilkiah, the high priest, found the book with the laws of Moses. It was the observance of these laws that had made his great-grandfather Hezekiah's reign so successful about 100 years earlier. Now they stirred and stimulated young Josiah to further religious reform, resulting in a fuller return to God's expressed will among His people (see verses 8-33).

Ezekiel's childhood occurred during Judah's return to God and His service, under the effective leadership of King Josiah. At the time of Josiah's fatal wound and consequent death following his unfortunate encounter with Pharaoh Necho at Megiddo in 609 B.C., Ezekiel was just reaching his teens.

Josiah's good example of faithfully serving the Lord was not duplicated by the kings who followed him on the throne. Politically Judah was beginning to experience the results of her apostasy foretold by the prophets Habakkuk and Zephaniah. Judah was sliding from independence to abject dependence and finally to total subjugation to Babylon during the reigns of Josiah's four successors.

The political dominance in the Near East during this period shifted from Assyria to Babylon. Nineveh's fall in 612 B.C. betokened Assyria's collapse, which was effectually sealed with the defeat of Pharaoh Necho, an ally of Assyria, at Carchemish on the Euphrates in 605 B.C. This introduced the unquestioned supremacy of Babylon as the dominant power in the Near East.

Late that same year, 605, Nebuchadnezzar attacked and took Jerusalem and made Judah subject to Babylon. Nebuchadnezzar took as booty part of the Temple vessels and young Hebrew captives to Babylon (see Dan. 1:1-3). Writing about this approximately 70 years later, Daniel titled Nebuchadnezzar king, although the capture of Jerusalem and the subjugation of Judah took place a few weeks before his father Nabopolassar's death.

To Ezekiel, 17 years old and slated for the priesthood, this was a heartbreaking tragedy. Seeing his country—God's chosen nation on earth—become subject to another nation hurt him deeply. And seeing some of the brightest Jewish youths taken to Babylon to be trained for Babylonian civil service filled him with grief.

But political disturbance with national humiliation did not end with this. Jehoiakim, although having sworn loyalty to Babylon, was an unstable vassal. After a reign of a little more than 10 disastrous years he died in ignominy, rejected of Heaven, unloved by his people, and despised by the rulers of Babylon, whose confidence he had betrayed. His son Jehoiachin followed him on the throne. But he was just as disloyal to his Babylonian overlord, Nebuchadnezzar, as his father had been. He rebelled, Jerusalem was besieged and captured, and after only three months he was removed from his throne. Together with 10,000 captives (see 2 Kings 24:14), he himself with his family was taken captive to Babylon. Among the captives was the priest Ezekiel.

For the Hebrew captives the days and years in Babylon idled away, filled with sorrow and regret. The psalmist pictured the exiles as saying: "By the rivers of Babylon we sat down and wept when we remembered Zion. There on the willow-trees we hung up our harps, for there those who carried us off demanded music and singing, and our captors called on us to be merry: 'Sing us one of the songs of Zion.' How could we sing the Lord's song in a foreign land?" (Ps. 137:1-4, NEB). The captives realized that their dismal fate had befallen them because of their disloyalty to God as a people.

But the Hebrews were not actual prisoners. They were free to live their own lives and go about their own business. They were also allowed to live with their own countrymen in colonies. Ezekiel was with a group of Hebrews living by the river Chebar about 50 miles north of Babylon (see Eze. 1:1-3).

Ezekiel shared his people's sorrow over his country's subjection to Babylon. For him captivity might have been doubly heavy since he knew that if he had been in Judah he could have begun his priestly service in the Temple, since he had now reached his thirtieth year. That desirable prospect did not beckon him in captivity. Possibly as these mournful thoughts floated through his mind "by the river Chebar, the heavens were opened," and he saw "visions of God" (verse 1).

After he had seen God, His Spirit entered into him, and God's prophetic commission came to Ezekiel in these words: "I send you to the people of Israel, to a nation of rebels, who have rebelled against me" (Eze. 2:3). God characterized the exiles as "impudent and stubborn." But whether or not they would heed God's word to them through His prophet, they were to know "that there has been a prophet among them" (verse 5).

Then the Spirit lifted Ezekiel up and took him to the exiles at Telabib by the river Chebar. But on his arrival he remained speechless among them for seven days (see Eze. 3:15). The reason for this muteness is not quite clear, but he was apparently overwhelmed (possibly by their attitude toward the conditions under which they lived) and reluctant to convey the Lord's horrifying message to them, a message of judgment, misery, and bloodshed.

In the country of Judah conditions went from bad to worse. Although Zedekiah, Jehoiachin's uncle and third son of Josiah to ascend the throne, had sworn loyalty to Nebuchadnezzar, he continued Judah's rebellion, exhausting Nebuchadnezzar's patience. Nebuchadnezzar decided to raze Jerusalem and thus deprive the Jews of their strongest fortress in order to quell their rebellious opposition and remove even figurative independence. To that end the Babylonian army laid siege to Jerusalem early in 588 B.C., about three and a half years after Ezekiel's call to the prophetic office.

On the morning of the very day the Babylonian armies began their siege, God spoke to Ezekiel and said: "Son of man, behold, I am about to take the delight of your eyes away from you" (Eze. 24:16). In other words, God told him his wife was about to die. And before the day ended his wife died. And God told him he must not even shed any tears over her death.

The death of his wife was Ezekiel's climactic tragedy. It topped both his pain of not having been able to minister as a priest in Solomon's magnificent Temple and his own country's loss of independence, which would soon end in complete subjugation to Babylon. And Ezekiel was an exile in the country that had shattered his dreams and destroyed his own nation. And still no crying!

In Ezekiel's "days it was customary for people to give spontaneous outward expression to inner emotion. But although Ezekiel was deeply devoted to his wife, he suppressed his grief and made no use of the traditional signs of mourning. . . . It was a symbol and sign to the people. At the fall of Jerusalem, the grief of the captives would be too deep for cries and tears; overwhelmed by the catastrophe, they would be stunned into silence (Eze. 24:15-27)" (Stephen Winward, *A Guide to the Prophets* [Atlanta: John Knox Press, 1976], p. 157).

And Ezekiel still had his prophetic commission from God. That had not been withdrawn. The very death of his wife was part of that message to his fellow captives. And so Ezekiel, whose name means "God strengthens," pursued his God-entrusted mission. It had never been easy. The exiles had never been cordial and receptive to his messages. God had warned him at the time of his call that his hearers would be stubborn and impudent rather than receptive. But until now Ezekiel had at least had one intimate friend—his wife. At all times she had been his solace, joy, and comfort—indeed, the delight of his eyes. Now she—his best friend—was gone.

In giving Ezekiel his commission, God had addressed him as "Son of man" (Eze. 2:1). By doing so, God wanted to encourage him.

Repeatedly (more than 90 times) God addressed Ezekiel in this way. In his vision Ezekiel had seen God in His overwhelming power and glory. "Son of man" expressed the contrast between God's omnipotence and the prophet's human weakness and frailty.

While Jesus lived on this earth as a man, "Son of man" was His favorite designation for Himself.[2] But Jesus was strong through the infilling of the Spirit. God wanted Ezekiel, though just a mortal, to become strong and sufficient for every need through the infilling of the Spirit. Realizing his weakness, Ezekiel would be more apt to rely on God's strength. And Ezekiel needed to be dauntless and strong, for

God was sending him, as He expressed it, "to the people of Israel, to a nation of rebels" (verse 3).

Ezekiel's prophecies were to be directed to Israel, and not specifically to Judah (see Eze. 2:3; 3:1, 4, 5, etc.). It was the "children of Israel" (Ex. 3:10, NKJV) that God brought out of Egypt and settled in Canaan. And not God's will, but transgression against God, led to the division into Israel and Judah.

The Assyrian Empire liquidated the kingdom of Israel and brought many of its people into Assyrian captivity. By the time of Ezekiel's prophetic ministry, Babylon had swallowed up the territory of the former Assyrian Empire. Judah was soon to experience the same fate. The captives from Israel and Judah and their descendants were all to be subjects of Babylon. In this way, in a sense, the 12 tribes had been reunited in captivity. They were all descendants of God's historical Israel, and so God, in all Ezekiel's prophecies, addresses all Jews both in exile and in Judea as Israel. In only one instance does Ezekiel name both Israel and Judah (Eze. 9:9). But he repeatedly speaks of Jerusalem, the capital of the original undivided Israel. God's messages through Ezekiel were for both Israel and Judah or descendants of the original Israel. For this reason Ezekiel speaks to Israel. Jeremiah likewise spoke of both Israel and Judah by calling them Israel.

In his prophecies after the overthrow of the kingdom of Judah, Ezekiel envisioned the restoration of all captive Hebrews—both Israelites and Jews. Together they were to constitute postexilic Israel. And the glorious promises he gave to Israel in the latter part of his book applied to regenerate and restored Israel.

Hardly any one of us has faced the triple tragedy that befell Ezekiel. As a teenager he saw his country lose its political freedom, starting along a path to complete political extinction. At about 25 years of age he was taken as a captive to the nation that was his own country's political overlord. This deprived him of the opportunity to serve as a priest in God's Temple at Jerusalem. And as a married man he lost the delight of his eyes at only 34 years of age.

For more than 20 years Ezekiel lived and prophesied among his down-in-the-mouth fellow-captives in Babylon. They did not care for his disheartening messages. But amid all his trials as God's spokesman to Israel Ezekiel clung tenaciously to his God.

"Circumstances have but little to do with the experiences of the soul. It is the spirit cherished which gives coloring to all our actions. A man at peace with God and his fellow men cannot be made miserable. Envy will not be in his heart; evil surmising will find no room there; hatred cannot exist. The heart in harmony with God is lifted above the annoyances and trials of this life" (Ellen G. White, *Testimonies*, vol. 5, p. 488).

Ezekiel experienced growth and triumph in the midst of triple tragedy.

---

[1] It is interesting to note that both John the Baptist and Jesus also began their public ministry at the age of 30 (see Luke 3:23).

[2] "Son of man" occurs more than 70 times in the four Gospels. In the Synoptic Gospels (Matthew, Mark, and Luke) it is always used by Jesus about Himself. In John's Gospel it is used by Jesus Himself in all but two cases (scornful persons account for these exceptions). "Son of God" occurs only 30 times in the Gospels, a little more than one third as often as "Son of man." In the Synoptic Gospels it is never used by Jesus about Himself; other people use it half the time, devils account for its other half, and an angel uses it once. In the Gospel of John "Son of God" is used half the time by Jesus and half by other people.

CHAPTER 2

GOD ON
HIS THRONE

Based on Ezekiel 1-3

In the vision that preceded his call to the prophetic office, Ezekiel saw the heavens opened and the chariot throne of God. But only after he had felt the hand of the Lord laid upon him and been filled with heavenly power for the discharge of his prophetic task did the vision unravel to him in installments.

Ezekiel first saw a stormy wind and a great cloud coming "out of the north" (Eze. 1:4). It was bright with fire flashing out from it continuously. Out of the storm cloud emerged four living creatures, each with four wings. Each of them had also four different faces: that of a man, a lion, an ox, and an eagle. John B. Taylor suggests that "these represented the highest forms of life to be found among the different realms of God's creation" (*Ezekiel* [Downers Grove, Ill.: Inter-Varsity Press, 1969], p. 55).

In Ezekiel 10, which closely parallels chapter 1, Ezekiel tells us that the living creatures were cherubim, or angels. (And angels are "ministering spirits" [Heb. 1:14] cooperating with Christ and the Holy Spirit in the salvation process among men. These creatures also appear around God's throne in Revelation 4.) When moving, these creatures never turned, but went straight forward in any direction. In their midst was something that looked like a burning fire. From this lightning issued forth continuously. The living creatures themselves also darted to and fro, like lightning.

As Ezekiel looked further, he saw a wheel by each living creature. They sparkled like chrysolite and appeared to intersect one another. They moved in any direction with the living creatures, either on land or in the air, for the same spirit moved both. The rims of the wheels were full of eyes, symbolizing that they were moved by intelligent forces. "For the spirit of the living creatures was in the wheels" (Eze. 1:21).

Above the heads of the living creatures a dome or firmament appearing like dazzling crystal seemed to stretch out. Above the dome was something looking like a throne of sapphire, and seated on it was a figure like a man. The different parts of the figure shone with the brightness and radiance of the different colors of the rainbow that surrounded the figure. This was the manifest glory of God that appeared to Ezekiel in vision.

By this vision Ezekiel joined several other Bible characters who were also granted theophanies. Joshua met the Lord in the person of a military commander outside Jericho (see Joshua 5:13, 14). To Isaiah standing in the portico of Solomon's Temple, the gate and the inner veil suddenly seemed to be withdrawn and he "saw the Lord sitting upon a throne" in the Holy of Holies (see Isa. 6:1). To Daniel, but not to those who were with him, the Lord appeared on the bank of the Tigris River clothed in linen with a belt of gold and face and eyes as flashes of lightning and flaming torches (see Dan. 10:4-7). Paul on the road to Damascus to apprehend followers of Jesus (or the Way, as nascent Christianity was first called) met Christ as a light from heaven speaking to him (Acts 9:3-7). On the island of Patmos, to which the apostle John had been banished "on account of the word of God and the testimony of Jesus," Christ appeared "like a son of man, clothed with a long robe and with a golden girdle round his breast; his head and his hair were white as white wool, white as snow; his eyes were like a flame of fire" (Rev. 1:9, 13-16).

When God called Moses to be the emancipator of the Israelites from bondage, He appeared to him as a burning bush (see Ex. 3:1-5). But as Moses continued to serve God, he came so close and became so intimate with God that God talked to Moses "face to face" (Deut. 34:10).

In trying to describe his vision of God Ezekiel used utmost reserve. He used words like "likeness" and "appearance" and even the phrase "the appearance of the likeness." He was aware that the symbols he saw were not the reality. He saw pictures that he found exceedingly difficult to describe in sharp and vivid detail. Heavenly realities go beyond all human understanding.

Ezekiel's symbolic language conveyed his awareness of overwhelming majesty, mystery, and glory. He sensed the truth that the apostle Paul later expressed when he wrote: "For now we see in a mirror dimly" (1 Cor. 13:12). The "covering that is cast over all peoples, the veil that is spread over all nations" (Isa. 25:7) had not yet been removed. Heavenly realities defy human understanding and elude our observation and exact description. Paul found himself in the same dilemma when he tried to relate what he had seen after having been caught up into the third heaven. In Paradise he had "heard things which cannot be put into words" (2 Cor. 12:3, 4, TEV).

The whole vision is one of movement. The wheels, the living creatures, the firmament, and the throne on the firmament are all in motion. God is going somewhere, and that is apparently the point of the vision. William H. Shea comments: "Commentators on this passage have noted and emphasized that this is a vision of the glory of God, which it certainly is. But they have only incidentally noted the motion involved in this vision. God and His glory are not oscillating idly back and forth in a vacuum. His movement is intentional and directional. He is the One who orders the wheels and the living beings to follow the direction in which they are to travel with the firmament and His throne" ("The Investigative Judgment of Judah," in A. V. Wallenkampf and W. R. Lesher, eds., *The Sanctuary and the Atonement* [Washington, D.C.: Review and Herald, 1981], p. 285).

In his vision Ezekiel saw God coming "out of the north" (Eze. 1:4). When this phrase or "from the north" refers to enemies coming against Israel, it refers to geographical direction (see Jer. 1:13, 14; 4:6; etc.). Babylon would soon bring final and total destruction to Judah from the north. Although located east of Judah, the enemies coming from the Tigris and Euphrates valleys always took a circuitous route that avoided the intervening desert and brought them to the inhabitants of ancient Canaan always from the north.

In Ezekiel's vision "out of the north" refers to God. The north is alluded to in the Bible as God's dwelling place. In rebelling against God in heaven, Lucifer said in his heart: "I will ascend to heaven; above the stars of God I will set my throne on high; I will sit on the mount of assembly in the far north" (Isa. 14:13). Jerusalem with Mount Zion was an earthly symbol of God's dwelling place: "Mount Zion, in the far north, the city of the great King" (Ps. 48:2).

In Ezekiel's vision God was moving out of His heavenly dwelling place. But Ezekiel does not tell us which direction God's chariot took in coming "out of the north." In chapters 8:4, 9:3, and 10:4, however, Ezekiel saw God in His Temple in Jerusalem. And in verses 18 and 19 he saw the glory of God, on His chariot throne (which he had seen in his vision in chapter 1), leaving the Temple in Jerusalem.

So in coming "out of the north" on His chariot throne God was evidently traveling to His earthly Temple in Jerusalem. "The principal point of the vision in the first chapter of Ezekiel is that God was in transit by means of His celestial chariot to the site of His earthly residence, His Temple in Jerusalem" *(ibid.,* p. 286). According to the date of Ezekiel's prophecies in Ezekiel 1:1, 2 and 8:1, God was to reside there for a period of 14 months.

But why did God come to His earthly Temple and what did He do while He was there? His presence in the Temple was already represented by His Shekinah glory resting over the ark of the covenant in the Most Holy Place.

But His real dwelling place was not His Temple in Jerusalem. He Himself says, "On high I dwell, and in holiness" (Isa. 57:15, NAB). Solomon called God's dwelling place "the heavens and the highest heavens" (1 Kings 8:27, NAB). Not even these can contain Him. The prophet Zechariah spoke of His dwelling place as "His holy habitation" (Zech.

2:13, NKJV), where He lives "in unapproachable light" (1 Tim. 6:16, NKJV), as Paul termed it. But on earth His presence was represented by the Shekinah glory in the Jewish Temple.

Apparently God came to His earthly Temple for a special, important work. "The messages given to the prophet, as recorded in the chapters spanning the gap between the visions of chapter 1 and of chapter 8, suggest that special work was of judgment, for that is the message they convey. In other words, Yahweh [Jehovah] sat in judgment upon His people in His Temple for some 14 months, according to the datelines connected with these visions, the contents of the visions themselves, and the nature of the messages given to Ezekiel during the interval between the two visions" *(ibid.,* pp. 286, 287).

God is not a prisoner confined to any particular space in His universe. His throne is not fixed, but mobile. His heavenly chariot is equipped with both wheels and wings. It can move in any direction at any time, and to any place. He is the independent and the supreme ruler of the whole universe and able to be in any place He chooses with His movable throne. And Ezekiel in vision saw God sitting in judgment upon His chosen nation before the ultimate destruction of Jerusalem and the nation by Babylon.

At the time Ezekiel received this vision it appeared to the exiles "that God was no longer in control. The plundering of the heathen nations at will was interpreted by many as though God no longer cared. The people failed to see the hand of God in the course of history. They were unaware of the fact that a divine, overruling purpose was at work in recent developments, as indeed it had been in all ages" *(The SDA Bible Commentary,* vol. 4, p. 577).

For a while Ezekiel had been affected by the thinking of the discouraged exiles. He mourned bitterly day and night and "was weighed down with sorrowful memories and troubled forebodings. . . . The prophet himself was a stranger in a land where ambition and cruelty reigned supreme. As on every hand he beheld tyranny and wrong, his soul was distressed, and he mourned day and night. But the symbols presented to him revealed a power above that of earthly rulers" (Ellen G. White, *Education,* p. 177).

"The wheellike complications that appeared to the prophet to be involved in such confusion were under the guidance of an infinite hand. The Spirit of God, revealed to him as moving and directing these wheels, brought harmony out of confusion; so the whole world was under His control. Myriads of glorified beings were ready at His word to overrule the power and policy of evil men, and bring good to His faithful ones" (White, *Testimonies,* vol. 5, p. 752).

This vision of God on His rainbow-enshrouded throne brought renewed courage to Ezekiel. He remembered that the rainbow was God's original sign of His covenant faithfulness and mercy on man and on "every living creature of all flesh that is on the earth" (Gen. 9:16, NKJV). To Ezekiel the bow over the throne was assurance that all was not lost. God's mercy was still over His nation, and salvation was still awaiting those who chose to accept it and abide by God's covenant. In the vision he had perceived an overruling power mightier than that of earthly rulers. Above the proud and cruel monarchs of Assyria and Babylon the God of mercy and truth was still enthroned.

Ezekiel realized that God was still in control. He had not forgotten His people. He still cared for them. He overrruled the events that affected nations as well as the experiences that come into the lives of all those who have committed themselves to Him.

To Ezekiel this realization was like a pleasant perfume pervading the atmosphere surrounding him. This awareness enabled him to proclaim joyfully God's message among his fellow captives, even though they at times would make it as uncomfortable as sitting "upon scorpions" (Eze. 2:6). Herbert May in *The Interpreter's Bible* (New York: Abingdon Press, 1956) observes that this threat "is most vivid to one who has lived in Palestine" (vol. 6, p. 78). The hearts of those among whom Ezekiel was to work were venomous as scorpions. The sting of a scorpion causes sharp pain, followed by numbness of limb with local swelling. Amid such uninviting conditions Ezekiel was to prophesy. The awareness that God is on His throne acted as a healing balm to Ezekiel's previously agitated mind. He joined the prophet Habakkuk in rejoicing that "the Lord is in his holy temple" (Hab. 2:20). That assured Ezekiel that ultimately all things would be right.

Without a doubt many of us today have been coping with the same problem that troubled Habakkuk and Ezekiel. We have been and are puzzled by what is happening. We see injustices perpetrated in many places, in the lives of both individuals and nations. With Habakkuk we are prone to cry, "How long, O Lord, will You permit this to go on without doing anything about it?"

We would like to set things right at once—immediately. We would balance the accounts right now, just as Habakkuk would. Some—in seeing this—are prone to believe that God has forsaken the world, as did the Jewish exiles in Babylon. They feel that the nations and the people have been left to handle things on their own.

The realization that God is still on His throne and will set everything right in due time will act as a healing balm to our disturbed souls, as it did to Habakkuk and Ezekiel. With Ezekiel we will remember that God does not engineer either wrongs or misfortunes to make life difficult. But we will recognize that at times He permits them to touch even the lives and experiences of His committed followers. We know that whatever God permits to come into a person's life may become a stepping-stone, rather than a stumbling block, provided his attitude toward God is right. Both a person's success and misfortune pivot on the individual's attitude toward God and His will. It is not primarily what happens, but rather a person's response to what happens, that determines whether or not the occurrence will become a boon or bane.

God has not abdicated from His rulership of the universe. He has not given up. He has abandoned neither His creation nor its people. He is aware of what is going on, and He cares for all. He cares for you and me. He knows us by name, and He vows: "I will not forget you. Behold, I have graven you on the palms of my hands; your walls are continually before me" (Isa. 49:15, 16).

CHAPTER 3

SOWING AND
REAPING

Based on Ezekiel 4-7

Ezekiel began his prophetic ministry by enacting several pantomimes at the command of God. These depicted the ensuing siege and destruction of Jerusalem, with the end of Judah as an independent nation and the Jews in Babylonian captivity. These were visible, outward acts that were to be seen as signs (see Eze. 4:3). Merely spoken presentations of what Ezekiel had seen in vision, however vivid, were unable to make the same powerful impression on his hearers. Visual images would reinforce the prophet's messages.

When the people saw Ezekiel's strange doings they would naturally ask him what his antics meant. In this way they opened the way for him to explain further what God intended to do.

Chapters 4 and 5 belong together. "They contain five dramatic actions, three having to do with the fate of Jerusalem, and two with the Exile. Ezekiel is told to draw on a brick a picture of Jerusalem under siege, and to set his face against it (Eze. 4:1-3), to eat rationed food and water (verses 9a, 10, 11, 16, 17), and to shave his hair with a sword and dispose of the hair in ways indicative of the fates of the people at the destruction of the city (Eze. 5:1-17). He . . . is ordered to eat food cooked in an unclean manner, even as the people of Israel will eat their food unclean among the nations (Eze. 4:12-15)" (May, *The Interpreter's Bible*, vol. 6, p. 85). All these pantomimes were messages of doom.

When Ezekiel had shaved off his hair and beard, God said: "This is Jerusalem; I have set her in the center of the nations, with countries round about her" (Eze. 5:5). About this Peter C. Craigie remarks: "Again, one must imagine the scene. The speaker of these dramatic words offers a strange spectacle: his head is now bald and his jaw shaven of its traditional beard. And when he says, 'This is Jerusalem,' he refers in a manner to himself; this stange and sheared person you see standing before you represents the sorry estate to which Jerusalem is coming. His dreadful message is not of Babylon, the city of the hated enemy, but of their own beloved capital city" *(Ezekiel* [Philadelphia: Westminster Press, 1983], p. 39). The prophet's actions declare that judgment is coming to Jerusalem because of her departure from God's will.

When God called Abraham to be His representative to a world engulfed in willful departure from His will, He did not leave him in Ur in Chaldea. In Abraham's day Ur was close to the Persian Gulf. Today it is halfway between Babylon and the Persian Gulf. He took him to Palestine, the crossroads of the ancient world. The caravan routes between the three most populous continents of the world—Asia, Africa, and Europe—converged in the small land area of Palestine. In this way Abraham and his descendants as God's representatives would come in contact with more people in Palestine than they could have reached in any other location of the ancient world.

In Abraham and his descendants "all nations on earth will be blessed, because you have obeyed me" (Gen. 22:18, NIV). These were God's words of approval and commendation to Abraham after he had taken his son Isaac to Mount Moriah to sacrifice him.

When the Israelites at the Exodus became a nation, God "set her in the midst of the nations and the countries all around her" (Eze. 5:5, NKJV). Doing this affirmed that God's purpose for Old Testament Israel was the same as it had been for Abraham and for his New Testament Christian church. Of it Jesus said: "You are the light of the world" (Matt. 5:14).

But God's purpose was fulfilled only occasionally, as during the days of David and the early part of Solomon's reign. At those times ancient Israel chose to be God's instrument for fulfilling His purpose. And the surrounding nations knew Israel was signally blessed by God. The queen of Sheba expressed the sentiments of the nations in her words to King Solomon, saying that "your wisdom and prosperity exceed the fame which I heard" (1 Kings 10:7, NKJV) and "because your God loved Israel and would establish them for ever, he has made you king over them, that you may execute justice and righteousness" (2 Chron. 9:8).

It was God's intention that the Israelites in Palestine should have been His instruments for extending His invitation to salvation to all the world. "To all the world the gospel invitation was to be given. Through the teaching of the sacrificial service Christ was to be uplifted before the nations, and all who would look unto Him should live. All who, like Rahab the Canaanite, and Ruth the Moabitess, turned from idolatry to the worship of the true God were to unite themselves with His chosen people. As the numbers of Israel increased they were to enlarge their borders, until their kingdom should embrace the world" (Ellen G. White, *Christ's Object Lessons*, p. 290).

As a nation Israel frustrated God's plan for them. They did not make God look good in the eyes of the heathen. Israel—and Judah—and Jerusalem should have been a continuous object lesson to the nations around them of the spiritual and material well-being that would accrue from obedience to God's will. But instead they became examples of misfortune that result from divergence from His will. God warned that in departing from Him Judah would reap "everlasting reproach and perpetual shame" (Jer. 23:40) from the nations around her.

With sorrow God said that Judah—and Israel—before her "rebelled against My judgments by doing wickedness more than the nations, and against My statutes more than the countries that are around her; for they have refused My judgments, and they have not walked in My statutes" (Eze. 5:6, NKJV). As a result, both "suffered the reproach of the nations" (Eze. 36:6).

Israel's calamity—with the fall of Jerusalem and all Judah before the Babylonians, with ensuing captivity—in the days of Ezekiel was the result of their own past doings. Ultimately, individuals as well as nations will inevitably reap what they sow. After Babylon had destroyed Judah, God said: "Son of man, when the house of Israel dwelt in their own land, they defiled it by their ways and their doings; their conduct before me was like the uncleanness of a woman in her impurity. So I poured out my wrath upon them for the blood which they had shed in the land, for the idols with which they had defiled it" (verses 17, 18).

This was the reason God allowed them to be scattered among the nations and dispersed throughout the countries. God judged them in accordance with their conduct and their deeds (verse 19), and permitted Babylon to discipline Judah (see Jer. 21:7; 37:17). God, like parents, disciplines because He loves His children. The apostle Paul expressed God's solicitude for His children by saying: "For the Lord disciplines him whom he loves, and chastises every son whom he receives" (Heb. 12:6).

Some friends of ours who had children of their own adopted a girl. The children grew up together. The parents were especially kind to this adopted child. But one day this girl came to her parents and said: "You don't love me as much as my sisters and brother. You never spank me." Because she was not disciplined in the same way as the others, she felt that she did not belong and that her parents did not love her as much as they did her siblings.

God said that He was against the Jews of Ezekiel's time. The reason for this was that Ezekiel's contemporaries were deliberate sinners (see Eze. 5:8, 9; 13:8, 9). It actually depends on a person whether God is for or against him. If a person goes in a direction opposite to that of God, He will naturally be against him. But if he goes in the same direction as God, He will naturally be for him. Therefore, when the Jews later repented of their former perverse ways and sided with God, He said: "For, behold, I am for you, and I will turn to you" (Eze. 36:9). The sum total of the wisdom of the ages is to find out where God is going, and then go with Him. To this we can add: "As the will of man cooperates with the will of God, it becomes omnipotent" (White, *Christ's Object Lessons*, p. 333). God wants to be for every one of us. But to enable Him to be for us, we must bring our lives and plans into line with His.

The universe, under an ethical God's control, operates by the law of like returns. It simply means that one reaps what one sows. Negatively stated, there is a law of just retribution, the *lex talionis*. Ezekiel in these chapters is pointing out that for the Jewish nation, the time for a just return had come.

The cause-and-effect relationship is just as inviolable in the spiritual realm as it is in the physical. "There are great laws that govern the world of nature, and spiritual things are controlled by principles *equally* certain. The means for an end must be employed, if the desired results are to be attained" (White, *Testimonies*, vol. 9, p. 221; italics supplied).

In the first part of chapter 6 Ezekiel pointed out the perversity of idol worship. When the Israelites came into Canaan, God warned them against it (see Lev. 26:27-30). He spoke to the "mountains of Israel" because they were centers of idolatrous worship of different forms (see Deut. 12:2; 2 Kings 17:10, 11; Jer. 2:20; 3:6, 23; Hosea 4:13). The efforts of neither Hezekiah nor Josiah (see 2 Chron. 31:1; 34:1-4) had effectively eradicated this form of idolatry. After every removal it quickly reasserted itself. For their violation of God's plan destruction would soon fall upon Judah. The tenor of the experience of the kingdom of Judah is expressed in 2 Chronicles 24:18. It reads: "And they forsook the house of the Lord, the God of their fathers, and served the Asherim and the idols. And wrath came upon Judah and Jerusalem for this their guilt."

Instead of a light and a source of blessing to the nations, Israel was "a scandal and a reproach" to the nations around it, and "all who pass by will see it. You will be an object of reproach and abuse, a terrible lesson to the nations around you" (Eze. 5:14, 15, NEB).

Chapters 6 and 7 reiterate the announcements of judgment pictorially presented in the two preceding chapters —chapter 6 in prose and chapter 7 in poetic form. The idol altars will be broken down and the dead Israelites will lie scattered around them (see Eze. 6:4, 5).

But even in that moment of destruction God will preserve a remnant (see verse 8). These faithful Israelites, while scattered among the nations, will remember their God and serve Him. The missionary activities the Israelites had refused to do as a nation, individual captives will now have an opportunity to perform among their heathen neighbors. To accomplish this neglected mission, only the best or most God-committed Jews were taken into Babylonian captivity (see Jer. 24:1-9).

Possibly it is more correct to speak not about God's punishment, but rather about results. God does not punish for the sake of inflicting suffering. Suffering results from violation of physical and spiritual laws. If one jumps off the roof of a high building, the jumper will get hurt when gravity pulls him too quickly back to the earth. Violation of the spiritual laws that govern the universe will likewise cause suffering.

However, suffering is not always a consequence of personal violation of God's laws. Sometimes it results from the accumulated effects of sin. This earth is the battlefield of the great controversy between God and Satan—and a battlefield is not a comfortable place for living. Nevertheless, all of us are living on it.

CHAPTER 4

THE MOST
DESPICABLE SIN

Based on Ezekiel 8-10

Exactly 14 months after his first vision (in Ezekiel 1), Ezekiel was sitting in his house with the elders of Israel (cf. Eze. 1:3; 8:1). At this meeting Ezekiel again sensed the hand of the Lord laid on him, imbuing him with heavenly power. In vision he was transported by the Spirit to the Temple in Jerusalem (see Eze. 8:3). Here he again saw the glory of God, which he had seen at his call to the prophetic office. God's destination in coming out of the north in that vision had been His earthly residence, the Temple in Jerusalem.

In vision Ezekiel was now shown four abominable forms of idol worship practiced at the Temple: the image of jealousy at the north gate, the most sacred and prestigious gate used by the king in coming to the Temple (verse 3); animal worship by 70 elders of the people (verses 9-12); worship of Tammuz (verse 14); and sun worship in the inner court of the Temple, open only to the priests and Levites (verse 16).

An idol, arousing the jealousy of God, stood at the north gate. Manasseh had erected a carved image of the Canaanite goddess Asherah in the Temple (2 Kings 21:7). This had apparently been removed (see 2 Chron. 33:15) but later restored. In the reformation by Josiah it was taken away and burnt at the Kidron brook (see 2 Kings 23:6). From Ezekiel's report it appears that Josiah's successors had made a new one and placed it again at the north gate.

Next, Ezekiel was led to a place where he could see 70 elders of Israel secretly bowing down to and worshiping animals portrayed on the walls. What doubly horrified Ezekiel was that the animals they worshiped as the gods of Israel were not even clean animals but loathsome beasts and reptiles. To these picture gods the elders were offering incense, although God had explicitly stated that incense must be offered only to Jehovah by the sons of Aaron (see 2 Chron. 26:16-18).

Ezekiel could hardly believe that he would see something like this in the Temple. But God told him: "You will see still greater abominations which they commit" (Eze. 8:13). So He took him to a place by the north gate of the Temple where women of Israel were worshiping Tammuz, a Sumerian god of vegetation, pastures, and flocks. At his annual death, vegetation dried up and died, but at his annual resurrection nature revived. Tammuz was worshiped by the surrounding nations for the power he supposedly exerted over nature. But not even this was all. God told Ezekiel again that there was more.

When the tabernacle and later Solomon's Temple were erected, God instructed His people that the entrance should face the east. This was so that worshipers would turn their backs to the rising sun in coming to the Temple to worship. In spite of this, the Israelites succumbed to sun worship, which was practiced by both Egyptians and Canaanites (see verse 16).

The 70 elders of the Temple in Jerusalem believed that "the Lord does not see us, the Lord has forsaken the land" (verse 12). In this way they felt free to engage in these heinous abominations of idol worship even in Solomon's beautiful Temple. These elders should have known that "the eyes of the Lord run to and fro throughout the whole earth" (2 Chron. 16:9). Nothing is hidden from Him. There are no secrets with God. Craigie observes that to "act as if there were is the height of folly. For human life is conducted on a stage like the interrogation room of a modern police department; the insiders cannot see out, but the observers can see and hear all that goes on inside the room" (Craigie, *Ezekiel*, p. 61).

The sins recorded in chapter 8 were mostly secret sins. They were not overt or open wrongdoing, but sins secretly engaged in. Their devotees hid from the public, and their practices were not known to the people at large. There are other sins that in themselves are just as abominable in God's sight, as are some secret sins. But they are not so devilish, since they are committed openly. Secret sins are indulged in under the pretense of good behavior or rightdoing. The secret sinner adds lying to his wrongdoing. He acts out his lie. He is a living lie.

Lying in all its different forms of deception, hypocrisy, etc., is pretense. Lying is the quintessence of sin or wrongdoing. It is also the most despicable and incurable. As a young man I enjoyed fishing. Most fish are slippery when they come out of the water. All newly caught fish slide through one's fingers easily. But once in lifting my fish trap in the spring I found an eel in it. It was nearly 30 inches long and had a round body about five inches in diameter. An eel has no fins and no scales, and is the most slippery fish I ever handled. A liar is slippery like an eel.

A thief, a fornicator, a murderer can be dealt with and hopefully restored to rectitude or rightdoing. But a liar is beyond help unless he chooses by the grace of God to change and become honest. A person who does wrong in secret is basically a liar. To his wrongdoing he wants to add an aura of rightdoing or righteousness. He does not admit to the wrongdoing for which he is reprimanded or apprehended. He staunchly maintains and asserts that none of the reports of his wrongdoing is correct. He insists on his innocence.

Jesus tells us that Satan is "the father of lies" (John 8:44)—not only of the spoken lie but also of the lived-out lie. He is the archpretender. He started it in Eden. When he came to Eve at the tree of knowledge he refused to sail under his own flag. Angels had warned Adam and Eve to be on the alert. They were told that Lucifer, one of the highest angels, had chosen to rebel and become Satan, the accuser. He had been ousted from heaven, and now would be unwearied in plotting to seduce them into joining his rebel forces.

Satan used the serpent as his decoy. At that time the serpent did not crawl on its belly, but had wings and could fly. It was an entrancingly beautiful animal, and also the wisest in God's garden. In flying, it presented a dazzlingly bright and fascinating picture. It was a thing of beauty and a delight to the eye. Sitting in the tree of knowledge eating the apparently delicious and harmless fruit, Satan began to talk to Eve. His voice was musical and pleasing. He praised Eve for her surpassing loveliness. This opened both Eve's ears and mind to his deceptive propositions, which ultimately resulted in her going against God's expressed will.

When Satan appeared to Jesus in the wilderness, he also came under the pretense of being someone else. He came in the guise of an angel from heaven in answer to Jesus' prayers. As a pretended ambassador from the Father, he declared that Jesus' fast was at an end. Pointing to some stones lying on the desert floor, Satan told Him to turn them into bread. Again Satan was a living lie. Hidden deception controls both mind and body. The acted-out lie is the total lie. The apostle Paul said that Satan himself "transforms himself into an angel of light" (2 Cor. 11:14). This is acted-out deception.

In his crowning attempt to seduce the loyal remnant into disobedience to God's word, Satan will go one better than that. When the faithful will be eagerly looking for Jesus as their Redeemer from this earthly pesthouse of sin and crime, Satan will impersonate Christ's second coming. The glory that will surround him will surpass anything human eye has ever seen. His appearance will resemble the portrayal of Christ in the book of Revelation. People will acclaim him as Christ with a shout of triumph: "Christ has come! Christ has come!" (see Ellen G. White, *The Great Controversy*, p. 624).

This is the acme of hypocrisy—of acted-out lying. The religious feigning to be Christ, the Saviour of the world coming for his own, when he is Satan!

Judas, the betrayer of Jesus, stooped to the level of

pretense. He led a mob to the Garden of Gethsemane to arrest Jesus. Finding Jesus there with the eleven, as he expected, he went up to Jesus and greeted Him with a kiss, while he placed his two hands on His shoulders as a disciple usually greeted a beloved rabbi. At this Jesus said to him: "Judas, would you betray the Son of man with a kiss?" (Luke 22:48).

It was not the kiss that Judas pressed upon the cheek of Jesus that was despicable. What is more beautiful than a kiss expressive of love and affection! It was not the kiss itself but the motive that prompted it that branded it devilish as a weed from hell. In the sight of God it is the motive prompting both word and deed that stamps them with either virtue or vice. Judas pretended to love Jesus. By pressing his kiss upon Jesus' cheek, he acted out his lie. He attempted to give an appearance opposite to what he really was.

An open sinner is less guilty in the eyes of God than one who professes to be righteous but sins in secret. Ananias and Sapphira lived double lives (see Acts 5:1-11). They did not forfeit life for reneging on their promise of giving the total sale price of their property to the church. They died for claiming to have given it all, while they had not done so. They died for scheming to look more generous than they were. They lied to God (verses 3, 4, 8, 9).

Jesus is adamantly against duplicity. He cursed the fig tree. It advertised fruit by its ostentatious show of foliage. A fig tree often produces fruit before its leaves open. So this full-leafed tree should have yielded figs, but it bore none. Therefore, it deceived the passersby. Jesus did not curse the fig tree for being barren, but for advertising what it did not deliver.

By the miracle of cursing the fig tree Jesus taught the inevitable doom of the hypocrite. "Christ never spoke so severely of anyone as of the hypocrites. Insincerity was the fault most personally offensive to him. The tree seemed to represent a hypocrite. It had leaves. There was fair outward show. It seemed to say, 'Come to me if you are hungry; I can refresh you.' And when Christ came he found the leaves were all it had to give. . . . Perhaps our Lord meant to picture Judas

Iscariot. Fairshowing as any disciple, but rotten-hearted. Let Pharisees learn, let Judas learn, let disciples learn, from the fig tree. . . . It is lying. . . . The hypocrite is corrupting. He is under the curse of God. There is no hope in this life or the next for the man who is consciously insincere" *(The Pulpit Commentary* [Grand Rapids: Eerdmans, 1974], vol. 15, p. 353).

The leaders of Jerusalem in the days of Ezekiel had sunk to the lowest level of sinfulness—the practice of secret sins, of leading double lives. Through their hidden desecration of the Temple they were driving God, its rightful occupant, away from His earthly abode (see Eze. 8:6). Because of this rank apostasy manifested in secret sins, God said: "I will deal in wrath; my eye will not spare, nor will I have pity" (verse 18). Execution of His purpose follows in chapter 9. All the inhabitants of Jerusalem were to be destroyed except those whom the angel of God had marked in their foreheads. These constituted but a remnant.

Ezekiel was appalled by the wholesale destruction he envisioned in chapter 9. Despite his apparently hard messages, he empathized with his suffering people. God had told him that He would make his head hard as adamant (see Eze. 3:9). Probably God had to do that to give Ezekiel, most likely a tenderhearted person, the ability and strength to endure what he had to face. Ezekiel apparently always had a heart of flesh that yearned for his people's safety and salvation.

After God had declared judgment on Jerusalem and His people in this investigative judgment of Judah, He departed from the Temple (see Eze. 10:18, 19). Almost two and a half years later the execution of the judgment began when the Babylonians began their final siege of Jerusalem in January, 588 B.C.

When Jesus, followed by His triumphal procession, approached Jerusalem on Palm Sunday, "it was not yet too late for Jerusalem to repent. The angel of mercy was then folding her wings to step down from the golden throne to give place to justice and swift-coming judgment. But Christ's great heart of love still pleaded for Jerusalem, that had scorned His mercies, despised His warnings. . . . If Jerusalem would but repent, it was not yet too late" (Ellen G. White, *The Desire of Ages,* p. 578).

The sentiment revealed by these words, spoken about Jerusalem in the days of Jesus, was equally applicable to Jerusalem housing Solomon's glorious Temple at this time of Ezekiel's ministry. There was still time to save the city and the Temple, provided the leaders would choose to follow God's word to them through the prophet Jeremiah.

CHAPTER 5

THE SURETY OF GOD'S WORD

Based on Ezekiel 11:1-13; 12; 24:1-14

In chapter 11 Ezekiel continued his description of Israel's moral condition, as seen in the vision of chapter 8. Now the Spirit took him to the east gate. Here he saw 25 men. These were "princes of the people" (Eze. 11:1), or civil leaders. Two of these Ezekiel knew—Jaazaniah and Pelatiah.

The Spirit told Ezekiel that "these are the men who devise iniquity and who give wicked counsel in this city" (verse 2). The "wicked counsel," *The Seventh-day Adventist Bible Commentary* suggests, was that the leaders in Jerusalem ignored "Jeremiah's warning concerning the impending destruction of the city, [and] continued to lay plans for building operations in the doomed city" (vol. 4, p. 611).

The Jews—probably under the influence of false prophets—did not believe that God would ever allow the Temple —His earthly dwelling place—to fall into the hands of heathen. They looked upon the Temple as a charm to protect the city and its inhabitants. Early in his ministry Jeremiah had warned: "Stop believing those deceitful words, 'We are safe! This is the Lord's Temple, this is the Lord's Temple, this is the Lord's Temple!'" (Jer. 7:4, TEV). His counsel from the Lord was: "Amend your ways and your doings, and I will let you dwell in this place" (verse 3).

Now in 591 B.C., more than two Babylonian invasions

later (with captives taken to Babylon both times), the Jews still felt just as secure in Jerusalem.

The civil leaders reasoned: "This city is a cooking pot, and we are the meat" (Eze. 11:3, NIV). As the meat in a kettle is safe and preserved from destruction by the fire, so the Jewish civil leaders felt fully safe from danger inside the city of Jerusalem. So their building activities went on as usual to execute the full restoration of the city after Nebuchadnezzar's siege at the time of Jehoiachin's and Ezekiel's captivity about six years earlier.

Because of their God-forgetting attitude, God told Ezekiel to prophesy against them. Jerusalem would not be their haven of refuge, as they self-sufficiently thought. God said: "This city shall not be your caldron [cooking pot], nor shall you be the flesh in the midst of it; I will judge you at the border of Israel; and you shall know that I am the Lord; for you have not walked in my statutes, nor executed my ordinances, but have acted according to the ordinances of the nations that are round about you" (verses 11, 12). While Ezekiel was still prophesying, Pelatiah fell down dead. At this the prophet was horror-stricken, fearing immediate destruction of all.

Chapters 12-24 deal specifically with Jerusalem and its impending fall. In the first part of chapter 12 Ezekiel is told to act out a parable of going into exile. His hearers were not only to hear his words but also to see them acted out (see Eze. 12:2). Hopefully the double-sense impression of both hearing and seeing would penetrate their rebellious shell and help them understand Jerusalem's precarious situation.

Ezekiel was to pack a rucksack with necessary possessions for survival. It would likely hold food, possibly an extra cloak to be used as a blanket, and minimal cooking utensils. He was to place the bag at the door of his house. At evening he was to pick up his baggage, dig a hole in the city wall, and carry his belongings through it out into the night with a muffled face. Of this performance God said: "I have made you a sign for the house of Israel" (verse 6).

When the exiles would ask him the next morning what his action of the preceding day meant (verse 9), God told him to tell them that his acted-out message "concerns the prince in Jerusalem and all the house of Israel who are in it" (verse 10). God through Ezekiel was foretelling that Zedekiah and many Israelites were to leave Jerusalem through a breach in the city wall, hoping to escape capture by the Babylonians (see 2 Kings 25:4).

After this, God told Ezekiel to act out the trembling fear of the inhabitants during the coming siege of Jerusalem (Eze. 12:17-20). Ezekiel ate bread and drank water while quaking in terror. The people saw the prophet spilling the water in trying to bring it to his lips and fumbling pieces of bread into his mouth. This pictured the mortal fear that would charac-terize the inhabitants of Jerusalem during the Babylonian siege.

The people seeing Ezekiel enact these scenes of terror did not believe that these calamities would befall their nation in their days. They congratulated themselves by saying: "Time goes by, and predictions come to nothing" (verse 22, TEV). But God ordered His spokesman to inform that He would put an end to that proverb. " 'Tell them instead: The time has come, and the predictions are coming true! . . . I, the Lord, will speak to them, and what I say will be done. There will be no more delay. In your own lifetime, you rebels, I will do what I have warned you I would do. I have spoken,' says the Sovereign Lord" (verses 23-25, TEV).

When Ezekiel spoke these words the besieging and conquering armies of Nebuchadnezzar were only a little more than two years away from Jerusalem. Closer in time than probably both Jeremiah and Ezekiel expected, even though both had foretold Jerusalem's fall and the end of the kingdom of Judah. Zedekiah had gone to Babylon in the fourth year of his reign to renew his oath of loyalty to Nebuchadnezzar (see Jer. 51:59). But that neither strength-ened his political position nor assured Nebuchadnezzar of his loyalty.

The Jews followed the common human tendency to explain away calamity. Possibly parents are responsible for having cultivated this notion in children. Mother or father may have told the small son: "If you do that, you'll get a spanking!" But when the adventurous young stripling did what the parents had forbidden, the consequences threatened by the parents did not ensue. Psychologists say that although the parents rarely relent, with possibly but one exception, the child remembers that once disobedience resulted in no unfavorable consequences. Therefore, the child is willing to risk his luck again and again. Criminals supposedly operate on the same basis. Others have gotten by, so I may also. Speeders on the highway operate by the same principle.

God, on the other hand, will never revoke His word. He will do what He says, but He does not always fulfill His word speedily. He patiently waits, hoping the sinner will come to himself and change his way, as did the prodigal (see Luke 15:11-32).

Many misinterpret God's deferment of immediate punishment and equate it with annulment of charges against them. This tends to nurture disregard for law. The wise man noted this by saying: "Because sentence against an evil deed is not executed speedily, the heart of the sons of men is fully set to do evil" (Eccl. 8:11).

After Eve realized she had eaten of the forbidden fruit, she expected something terrible to happen to her immediately. God had told Adam and Eve that they would die if they ate of the tree of knowledge. But nothing harmful had happened to her. So the serpent, not God, must have been right. Eve "felt no evidence of God's displeasure, but on the contrary realized a delicious, exhilarating influence, thrilling every faculty with new life, such, she imagined, as inspired the heavenly messengers" (Ellen G. White, *Patriarchs and Prophets*, p. 56).

Eve, like many even today, concluded that eating of the forbidden fruit did not harm her. She did not realize that if it had not been for Jesus stepping into the breach immediately to preserve her, her death would have occurred instantly.

Particularly in hospitals, we have emergency generators. These automatically click in to produce needed electrical power for light and other necessities the moment the inflowing electrical current stops. Before God created the world He had made provision that in case of sin, Adam and Eve and their descendants would not abruptly die if they violated the law of life. The plan of salvation, made before the foundation of the world, would instantly spring into action. It would preserve sinners from instant death. God chose humans to be saved through Jesus Christ "before the creation of the world" (Eph. 1:4, NIV; cf. 1 Peter 1:20).

At the time Adam and Eve ate the forbidden fruit they did not know about this covenant of grace. God unveiled it to them after their sin (see Gen. 3:15). Because of this covenant of grace made between the Father and the Son, Adam and Eve continued to enjoy life, although they merited death. "As soon as there was sin, there was a Saviour" (Ellen G. White, in *Review and Herald,* Mar. 12, 1901). "Christ, the Son of God, stood between the living and the dead, saying, 'Let the punishment fall on Me. I will stand in man's place. He shall have another chance' " *(The SDA Bible Commentary,* Ellen G. White Comments, vol. 1, p. 1085).

Today many a sinner, like Adam and Eve at the time of their transgression, does not know that his life is spared because of Christ's sacrifice.

God provided this covenant of grace so that Adam and Eve would have an opportunity to repent and change their attitude toward Him and His will under the promptings of the Holy Spirit. This plan is still operative and gives physical life to both saint and sinner. Those who refuse to avail themselves of this time of grace by accepting salvation through Jesus Christ will ultimately die the second or eternal death. "Against every evildoer God's law utters condemnation. He may disregard that voice, he may seek to drown its warning, but in vain. It follows him. It makes itself heard. It destroys his peace. If unheeded, it pursues him to the grave. It bears witness against him at the judgment. A quenchless fire, it consumes at last soul and body" (White, *Education,* pp. 144, 145).

God's every pronouncement of impending or ultimate judgment is an invitation to repentance. By pointing out the disastrous consequences of a certain course, God hopes man will change his way and his attitude toward Him and His will. God's judgment is rooted in man's past wrongdoing. It is just the unavoidable effect of a certain cause. The calamity that was to befall Jerusalem and its inhabitants resulted from their own evil, rather than growing out of the will and counsel of God.

God gave these messages through Ezekiel, seconding Jeremiah's prophecies, to enable the Jews to save both the city of Jerusalem from destruction and its people from death. They could do that by surrendering to the Babylonians. This was God's advice to them through Jeremiah: "Behold, I set before you the way of life and the way of death. He who stays in this city shall die by the sword, by famine, and by pestilence; but he who goes out and surrenders to the Chaldeans who are besieging you shall live and shall have his life as a prize of war" (Jer. 21:8, 9). For Jerusalem "shall be given into the hand of the king of Babylon, and he shall burn it with fire" (verse 10).

The prophecies of Jerusalem's imminent fall were God's call to His people to repent of their rebellious ways. Even at that late hour it was not too late to save both their lives and the city from destruction. God desired neither the death of the people nor the destruction of the city. He wanted to save both. But if they stubbornly persisted in their ways, there was nothing He could do except agonize over their destruction.

Hosea, centuries earlier, had expressed God's sorrow in these words, when His people persisted in their wayward paths leading to death. "How can I give you up, O Ephraim! How can I hand you over, O Israel! How can I make you like Admah! How can I make you like Zeboiim! My heart recoils within me, my compassion grows warm and tender" (Hosea 11:8).*

About two and a half years after Ezekiel had foretold the imminent final fall of Jerusalem in chapter 12, on a day in early January of 588 B.C., Jerusalem's doom struck. The predictions by Ezekiel and Jeremiah, which the Jews had said would "come to nothing" (Eze. 12:22, TEV), were being fulfilled. Nebuchadnezzar's forces began their siege of Jerusalem. Though delayed in the eyes of the Jews, it had come in God's own time. The cooking pot—Jerusalem—was corroded and the meat cooking within it was spoiled. The pieces of flesh inside it—all the inhabitants of Jerusalem—were poured into the fire. They could not escape. All would suffer in the fire of the Babylonian siege. The red-hot cauldron stood on the fire until the filth and rust had melted.

With sorrow God declared: "Its rust is your filthy lewdness. Because I would have cleansed you and you were not cleansed from your filthiness, you shall not be cleansed any more till I have satisfied my fury upon you" (Eze. 24:13).

"The appalling sufferings, undergone by God's people from 588 B.C. onwards, in the siege and exile, were due to their unwillingness to allow God to deal with them much earlier on in their history of disobedience. And now the sentence has been passed, the moment of execution has come. Nothing can turn it back, I the Lord have spoken. His decision and His word and His action are alike irrevocable" (Taylor, *Ezekiel*, p. 180).

For us today the fulfillment of God's word is equally sure. The antediluvians taunted Noah for preaching a flood. To them that was impossible because there had never before been a flood. Many today scorn the thought of Christ's second coming. But the scornful will soon be confounded by Christ's return to this earth as King of kings and Lord of lords to take His people to the mansions He has prepared for them. The redemption of the saved from this world of sin will mean destruction to those who have refused to believe His word and accept Him as their Saviour.

---

*Admah and Zeboiim were cities of the plain destroyed with Sodom and Gomorrah (see Deut. 29:23; cf. Gen. 14:8; 19:27-29).

C H A P T E R 6

SELF-DELUDED
LEADERS

Based on Ezekiel 13; 21:25-27; 22:23-31

The nation of Israel came into existence at the initiative of God. At the Exodus it was God who decided the Israelites were to leave Egypt. He called Moses to be the executor of His plan.

Moses responded to God's call and received guidance from God. He marched the hordes of Israel out of Egypt at the time God chose. And Moses did not decide where to go. God Himself led them. He "went before them by day in a pillar of cloud to lead them along the way, and by night in a pillar of fire to give them light, that they might travel by day and by night" (Ex. 13:21).

The cloud led them across dreary, desert-like land to a narrow gorge by the Red Sea. Rocks or mountains bordered their camping place on both north and south. As a man Moses, trained in Egyptian military science and strategy, would never have chosen such a place of encampment. But this place was God's choice, not his, and so he had no qualms about it. Tired after marching, the crowds settled down for a much-needed night's rest.

As they were retiring they began to hear rumblings from the west. Before long, they realized that the noise betokened the approach of the Egyptian army in pursuit of their slaves. At this realization the people became unreasonable and desperate. Frantic with fear, they blamed Moses for leading them out into the desert to die.

Moses felt no fear, knowing that God had led him and his people to this place. He told the people: "Do not be afraid. Stand still, and see the salvation of the Lord, which He will accomplish for you today. For the Egyptians whom you see today, you shall see again no more forever. The Lord will fight for you, and you shall hold your peace" (Ex. 14:13, 14, NKJV).

Then God moved the cloud, which had gone before them as a guide, behind them, separating them from the Egyptians. To the Israelites, the cloud then turned into a light, but to the Egyptians it was darkness. Then Moses, at the command of God, told the Israelites to go forward. As they stepped into the waters of the Red Sea, a way of escape opened up to bewildered Israel. In the radiance of light of day from the cloud they crossed the Red Sea on dry land during the night. When the Egyptians the next morning tried to follow them, they perished in the returning waters. It was not Moses who saved the Israelites from annihilation by the oncoming Egyptian army. It was God. Moses just trusted God and carried out His orders.

God had hand-picked Moses to be Israel's emancipator in the Exodus from Egypt. He was followed by Joshua, also selected by God, to bring the people across the Jordan and lead in the conquest of the Promised Land. The judges followed.

Some were disloyal to God. Samson, for example, chose not to be faithful to his call. Others, like Samuel, were God's men. The judges, like Moses and Joshua before them, were to be directed by God in leading Israel along God's path.

It was never God's plan that Israel should have a king (see 1 Sam. 8; Hosea 13:11). But God permitted them to exercise their free choice. He selected their first three kings. Even during the monarchy it was His desire to be Israel's real ruler. God planned to convey His will for His people through His spokesman or prophet. He in turn was to transmit it to the king. Even the Israelite monarchy was to be a theocracy.

The difficulty of this arrangement became immediately

evident during the reign of Saul, the first king. It was humiliating for Saul and every succeeding monarch to receive God's direction through a subject. Throughout the entire monarchy, whether in Israel or Judah, this plan created tension between the king and the prophet.

On the other hand, there was no comparable rupture between the kings and the priests. The Levitical priests were officials or servants of the Israelite state or economy in both the nation of Israel and Judah. So they usually cooperated with kings. The prophets, on the other hand, were free-lancers, belonging to neither the state nor the king. They were independent spokesmen for God and responsible and accountable only to God for faithfully proclaiming His plan and will irrespective of its acceptance.

The prophets were called by God to guide the nation along the path of His will through the executive authority of the king. The system usually did not work well. At times when the king followed the prophet's advice it brought great glory to God (see Isa. 36; 37). The tension between king and prophet was vicious during the reign of Zedekiah, the last king of Judah.

Zedekiah came to the throne of Judah at the dethrone-ment of his nephew Jehoiachin. Having been made king by Nebuchadnezzar, he swore allegiance to him. But he was an unreliable vassal. With other kings in the area he at times discussed and plotted rebellion against Babylon (see Jer. 28:1-4). In the fourth year of his reign—the year the false prophet Hananiah tried to stir up false hope of an early end of the captivity (see verses 5-17)—Zedekiah journeyed to Babylon to reassure Nebuchadnezzar of his continued loy-alty (see Jer. 51:59).

Zedekiah was king and nominal leader of Judah. But he was not a leader. Instead of leading, he was led by his princes (see Jer. 38:4, 5, 14-24). If Zedekiah was a leader at all, he was a leader in rushing the whole nation into even greater disregard of God's laws and will.

More than a year before Nebuchadnezzar's forces started their siege of Jerusalem, Ezekiel, in Babylon with the other exiles, bewailed Zedekiah's spineless wickedness in these words: "O unhallowed wicked one, prince of Israel, whose day has come, the time of your final punishment" (Eze. 21:25). Ezekiel, like all true prophets, could see what was going to happen in the future. The royal crown would pass from Judah. He said: "A ruin, ruin, ruin I will make it; there shall not be even a trace of it" (verse 27). Zedekiah's sentence was his loss of kingship and the end of the Jewish monarchy.

Ezekiel's portrayal of the priests, princes, alleged prophets, and even the common people is a picture of active wickedness. They were all rebels against God and His will. Through the inspiration of the Spirit, Ezekiel wrote about Judah and its people: "Again the word of the Lord came to me: 'Son of man, say to the land, "You are a land that has had no rain or showers in a day of wrath." There is a conspiracy of her princes within her like a roaring lion tearing its prey; they devour people, take treasures and precious things and make many widows within her. Her priests do violence to my law and profane my holy things; they do not distinguish between the holy and common; they teach that there is no difference between the unclean and the clean; and they shut their eyes to the keeping of my Sabbaths, so that I am profaned among them. Her officials within her are like wolves tearing their prey; they shed blood and kill people to make unjust gain. Her prophets whitewash these deeds for them by false visions and lying divinations. They say, "This is what the Sovereign Lord says"—when the Lord has not spoken. The people of the land practice extortion and commit robbery; they oppress the poor and needy and mistreat the alien' " (Eze. 22:23-29, NIV).

The conflict between Jeremiah and the king and princes furnished fertile soil for pseudoprophets. They claimed to speak for the Lord. In reality they prophesied "out of their own minds" (Eze. 13:17). God said about them: "You have profaned me among my people for handfuls of barley and for pieces of bread, putting to death persons who should not die and keeping alive persons who should not live" (verse 19).

Jeremiah, of course, did not curry favor with the king and princes. He was not a hireling, but a steward for God. As such he counted himself expendable. With the gloomy future painted by Jeremiah and Ezekiel, most of the Jews preferred to listen to good news of peace (see verse 10) from the false prophets. False prophets were found in both Judah and captivity and made the work of God's true messengers difficult.

These lulled the people into a false sense of security by assuring them that theirs was a time of peace. John B. Taylor says: "It is a common failing for preachers to want to speak pleasing and appealing words to their people, but if they are to be true to their calling they must be sure to receive and to impart nothing but God's clear word, irrespective of the consequences. When church leaders encourage their people in sub-Christian standards or unbiblical ways they make themselves doubly guilty" (*Ezekiel*, p. 122).

Nebuchadnezzar's assault, with the resultant fall of Jerusalem and the end of the kingdom of Judah as a sovereign nation, came as a blow to the people. They were unprepared for it mentally, physically, and spiritually.

God had been calling for men to prepare His people for it. But with sorrow God said: "O Israel, thy prophets are like the foxes in the deserts. Ye have not gone up into the gaps, neither made up the hedge for the house of Israel to stand in the battle in the day of the Lord" (verses 4, 5, KJV).[1] A year or so later God again expressed His disappointment by saying: "I sought for a man among them, that should make up the hedge, and stand in the gap before me for the land, that I should not destroy it: but I found none" (Eze. 22:30, KJV).

As the vineyard in the Bible often symbolizes God's chosen people (see Isa. 5:1-7; cf. Matt. 21:33), so the hedge surrounding it symbolizes His law. God's ancient people "were hedged about by the precepts of His law, the everlasting principles of truth, justice, and purity. Obedience to these principles was to be their protection, for it would save them from destroying themselves by sinful practices" (White, *Christ's Object Lessons*, pp. 287, 288).

But instead of presenting God's word to the people the false prophets endorsed their futile wishes for tranquillity and presented lying lullabies of peace. Ezekiel called these a wall[2] "daubed with untempered morter" (Eze. 13:14, KJV; cf.

verses 10, 12, 15, KJV). These prophets reasoned as the scoffers described by Isaiah who "made a treaty with death and reached an agreement with the world of the dead" by depending "on lies and deceit" to keep them safe (Isa. 28:15, TEV). They trusted their security to lies assuring themselves that no harm would touch them. But the scoffers met unexpected death. Their fallacious hopes did not come true. Neither did the expectations of the false prophets and their followers at the fall of Jerusalem.

For the ancient Jews the fall of Jerusalem and the end of the kingdom of Judah was the day of the Lord (see Zeph. 1:7, 14, 18; 2:2). This is the time when God intervenes in human affairs to execute judgment on evildoers. The destruction of impenitent Jerusalem was a symbol of the calamity that will overtake the whole world at the end of time. So from the destruction of ancient Jerusalem our thoughts pass to a wider judgment—to the time when God will subdue the nations of the earth and establish His own kingdom.

Ours is the time when human history is about to enter the period identified in the Bible as the day of the Lord. The day of the Lord climaxes in the second coming of Jesus. But this is immediately preceded by the seven last plagues (see Rev. 16). That is the last ordeal the redeemed will pass through before their deliverance from this sin-infected planet. The prophet Daniel speaks of it as "a time of trouble, such as never has been since there was a nation till that time." But he adds, "But at that time your people shall be delivered" (Dan. 12:1).

Today God's true followers, scattered throughout the world and found in every belief system, are ill-prepared to "stand in battle in the day of the Lord" (Eze. 13:5). God is anxious to make all truehearted believers ready for that great and terrible day. To that end He is calling upon every disciple to help repair the breach in His hedge of love, erected around His people. He wants every knowledgeable follower to be a "repairer of the breach" (Isa. 58:12).

There are many breaches or gaps in God's hedge of Ten Commandments today. Many are flagrantly violated, as for instance the seventh (see Ex. 20:14) enjoining sexual purity.

Violation of the ninth, bidding honesty (see verse 16), is still more common. Truthfulness is lightly regarded today despite God's declaration that there will be no liars in heaven (see Rev. 21:27; 22:15). And the fourth, decreeing observance of the seventh-day Sabbath (Ex. 20: 8-11), not just a sabbath, is commonly ignored by the whole Christian community. The prophet Isaiah, in ordering His people to teach the whole law, said that "if you turn back your foot from the sabbath, from doing your pleasure on my holy day, and call the sabbath a delight and the holy day of the Lord honorable; if you honor it, not going your own ways, or seeking your own pleasure, or talking idly; then . . . I will feed you with the heritage of Jacob your father" (Isa. 58:13, 14).

God gave His directions in the Ten Commandments to be not a burden, but a guide for comfortable and safe living: ". . . for our good always that he might preserve us alive" (Deut. 6:24). Before the seven last plagues begin to fall, God desires all of us to join in repairing the breaches in His hedge, and bring all His people, even the straying sheep, inside His sheepfold. Those inside the hedge will be protected from the ravages of the plagues.

"In obedience to God's law, man is surrounded as with a hedge and kept from the evil. He who breaks down this divinely erected barrier at one point has destroyed its power to protect him; or he has opened a way by which the enemy can enter to waste and ruin" (Ellen G. White, *Thoughts From the Mount of Blessing*, p. 52).

Today, as in the time of Ezekiel, God is looking for true leaders. Men like Ezekiel and Moses, who faithfully followed God's directions, not deluded ones like the false prophets, who spoke lies and prophesied "out of their own minds." Faithful men and women who trust the Human-Divine Teacher and gladly follow Him, remembering His words in John 8:29: "I always do what is pleasing to him [the Father]."

---

[1] "Hedge" is translated from the Hebrew word *gader*.

[2] "Wall" in these verses is translated from two other Hebrew words different and distinct from the Hebrew *gader*.

CHAPTER 7

INDIVIDUAL RESPONSIBILITY

Based on Ezekiel 14:12-23; 15; 18; 33:1-20

These passages of Scripture deal primarily with a person's responsibility before God. But if a person has no authority to decide and to act, he cannot justly be held responsible, because responsibility or accountability rests on commensurate authority or freedom. Only the person who possesses such freedom of choice and action can be held responsible.*

In Creation's morning God Himself gave to Adam and Eve, the progenitors of the human race, such freedom. He led them to the tree of knowledge and told them that they must not eat of its fruit. They were allowed to eat the fruit of every other tree in the garden, but the fruit of this tree they must leave alone.

Both Adam and Eve received the right and ability to think and act as individuals. If they would go contrary to His will, God told them that dire consequences would ensue. But God did not make it impossible for them to do so. It was within the choice of each to follow or disregard God's expressed will. Freedom of choice was not a communal gift, or even a gift given to a family as a unit. It was, and still is, a personal or individual endowment given to each member of the human race by God Himself.

In chapter 14 Ezekiel tells us that hypocritical leaders

came to him to find out God's will (see verse 7). Apparently they were hoping that they would be spared death when God's punishment would fall upon Judah, because of the righteous still among them. Through the Holy Spirit Ezekiel read their hearts. He saw that each had an idol in his heart, or that something took precedence in his thinking and affection over finding and doing God's will (see verse 4). Such inquirers God sets His face against, and will even cut off from among His people (see verses 7 and 8). Hundreds of years earlier wise King Solomon had written: "If anyone turns a deaf ear to the law, even his prayers are detestable" (Prov. 28:9, NIV). The request of these Jewish leaders was detestable to God.

Those who refuse to believe the truth will inevitably become victims of a lie. The apostle Paul wrote: "As they did not like to retain God in their knowledge, God gave them over to a debased mind" (Rom. 1:28, NKJV). And again: "They refused to love the truth and so be saved. Therefore God sends upon them a strong delusion to make them believe what is false" (2 Thess. 2:10, 11).

The mind is not a vacuum. If a person refuses to accept and permit truth to lodge in it, then it will be filled with error.

These elders, like the majority of the Jews, insisted on going their own way rather than God's. In this way God Himself could do nothing for them. Nor could anyone else.

To understand truth, we must be willing to follow revealed light. From a person who wants to practice truth nothing is withheld (see John 7:17). Crudely we say: "Don't throw pearls before swine." God chooses not to reveal truth that will be trampled underfoot by those who do not desire to apply it. God reserves His illumination for such who are willing to walk in His ways. A refusal to obey revealed truth prohibits further understanding of the divine will. God's word to these Jewish hypocrites was forthright: "Even if Noah, Daniel, and Job were in it [the land], as I live says the Lord God, they would deliver neither son nor daughter; they would deliver but their own lives by their righteousness" (Eze. 14:20).

Possibly these elders knew Daniel, just mentioned by

God, and were thinking of him. They knew that the lives of the wise men of Babylon were spared because of Daniel's and his companions' presence in their midst (see Dan. 2:12, 19, 24-28). So why should God not save them—Jews by blood—just as readily as He saved heathen Babylonians, because some good Jews were in their midst? They also remembered that Noah had been instrumental in saving his whole family.

They may also have thought back to the beginnings of Hebrew history and remembered Abraham and his intercession for the cities of the plain. Sodom, Gomorrah, Admah, and Zeboiim would all have been spared from destruction by fire, as Abraham pressed his request before God, if but 10 righteous people would have been found in them (see Gen. 29:23).

During World War II we heard stories from Europe of miraculous protection of Christian believers. Non-Christians felt safer in their presence, and at times of particular danger they would seek the company of committed Christians, because they believed their God would protect them.

Unbelievers have at times been safe and secure physically because of Christians among them. But when it comes to eternal salvation no one will be saved by association. Salvation depends on personal fellowship with God.

But the Jews in the days of Ezekiel maintained they were not responsible for their moral shortcomings. They conceded that they were not what they should be, but they blamed their parents and forefathers for this. They epitomized their excuses in the proverb "The fathers have eaten sour grapes, and the children's teeth are set on edge" (Eze. 18:2; cf. Jer. 31:29, 30).

Ezekiel took issue with this. He condemned their excuses. In chapter 18 he shows emphatically that the soul that sins "shall die" (verse 4), while the "righteous, he shall surely live, says the Lord God" (verse 9). This is also true of a righteous son of a wicked father. "When the son has done what is lawful and right, . . . he shall surely live" (verse 19). The reverse is also true (verses 10-13).

When a righteous man turns to wickedness "and commits iniquity" "he shall die" (verse 24). But a wicked man who turns away from his wickedness "shall surely live; he shall not die" (verse 21).

God finds "no pleasure in the death of any one" (verse 32). He who is life wants everyone to enjoy life. And so His plea to every person is to turn to the path of life "and live."

In today's urbanized areas mud is seldom seen. As a child and young man I lived and grew up in the country, and we had no scarcity of mud. In the spring there was mud everywhere. As children we made wonderful creations out of mud. The simplest were mud cakes or mud loaves. But we would also form animals out of mud: horses and cows, carefully molded out of the soft mud. Then we set them up to dry in the sun. If an elder brother would come by and disdainfully kick our mud creations into smithereens, we were heartbroken. After all, they were our creations, and therefore valuable to us.

Even the lowest human being is valuable to God. And no one was born into this world to die. Death was designed only "for the devil and his angels" (Matt. 25:41). Every human born into this world was originally to live and grow in health and happiness. That's the reason it hurts God even today to see us—or anyone—turn toward a path that He knows will lead to unhappiness and unnecessary sickness and premature death and ultimately to eternal death.

Every human being was "created in Christ Jesus for good works" (Eph. 2:10). But the Jews in the days of Ezekiel had departed from God's intended good works. About 50 years later the prophet Zechariah said that these Jews were not even willing to listen to God's will for them. Rather, "they refused to pay attention; stubbornly they turned their backs and stopped up their ears. They made their hearts as hard as flint and would not listen to the law or to the words that the Lord Almighty had sent by his Spirit through the earlier prophets" (Zech. 7:11, 12, NIV). And thus many of these reaped destruction at the fall of Jerusalem to Nebuchadnezzar.

God gave His laws to man for his good. Moses expressed it this way: "The Lord commanded us to do all these statutes, to fear the Lord our God, for our good always, that he might preserve us alive" (Deut. 6:24). The apostle Paul concurs that the commandment "was intended to bring life." But then he regretfully added that it "actually brought death" (Rom. 7:10, NIV). What was given for a person's good turned out to bring disaster and death.

Today just about all houses are wired for the use of electricity. No one would like to be without the convenience of electricity. With it we can take advantage of just about all modern conveniences and vicariously participate in numerous pleasures. Electricity makes life easier, if it is used with understanding. But stop for a moment. What would happen to you if you were taking a bath and an electric appliance that you had previously plugged in and turned on fell into the water by accident? You would be electrocuted instantly. Even though death was not the purpose for electricity in your home (its purpose was to make life easy and comfortable), using it incorrectly may make it a means of death.

We are not born into this world in groups. Each person comes into this world alone. Even twins are born one at a time. So every person is born singly into the kingdom of God, not in congregations, denominations, or churches. And after he/she is born into the kingdom of God, each person is ultimately responsible for his lasting saving faith relationship with God. Not even Noah, Daniel, and Job could bring eternal salvation to another. Receiving and keeping the gift of salvation is a personal responsibility.

That does not mean, however, that another person cannot facilitate or make another person's salvation easier, or contribute to another person's eternal damnation. If he is instrumental in causing "one of these little ones who believe in me to sin," Jesus said, "it would be better for him to have a great millstone fastened round his neck and to be drowned in the depth of the sea" (Matt. 18:6). A facilitator of a person's eternal loss will obviously not be held guiltless (see Matt. 23:13-15). And those who turn people toward righteousness and salvation shall shine "like the stars for ever and ever" (Dan. 12:3). Ezekiel was God's watchman among the exiles in Babylon to help them find and walk in the way of salvation.

Until a couple decades ago, many states in the United States with large forest areas maintained lookout towers. These were manned by rangers, particularly during the summer months while danger of forest fires existed. Male college students often accepted such a ranger assignment for the summer. Newly married student couples also would do so. These fire lookout towers were usually located on some high elevation far out in the forest areas.

These forest rangers were not fire fighters. They lived in these lonely outposts just to watch for and immediately report any possible forest fire or omen that might betoken imminence of one. If a fire would appear, fire fighters would be sent in either by land or as smoke jumpers by helicopters to put out or limit the spread of the fire. Today organized fire protection is even more sophisticated. In the United States only a very small percentage of woodlands lack any such protection.

Cities in Bible times were walled. But outside the city walls the inhabitants of the city would attend to their daily tasks of raising grains and fruit by farming the land beyond the city walls. To be able to attend to their work efficiently during uncertain times, the people of the city assigned certain men to be watchmen, to report the approach of any enemy or approaching danger. These watchmen were usually posted in watchtowers on the city wall. The ancient Jews also had wilderness watchtowers.

The responsibility of these watchmen was to report the approach of any enemies or thieves. At the appearance of anything suspicious, these watchmen would sound a warning by a trumpet, so that the people might be able to seek refuge and safety inside the city walls.

These watchmen were not soldiers. Their task was to alert the people of the city of their danger, so that they might resort to safety. They were like our forest rangers in fire lookout towers.

God told Ezekiel that He had called him to be a watchman on the symbolic walls of Zion among the exiles in Babylon. The exiles were now God's Israel. As the forest ranger in his fire lookout tower was a lonely individual, so

Ezekiel, as God's watchman, even though he would live among his own people, would be spiritually lonely. Ezekiel, as God's prophet, was destined to become "a lonely figure who [was] committed to the task of standing apart from his fellow-men in order to keep a constant vigil and warn his people of dangers that [lay] ahead" (Taylor, *Ezekiel*, p. 213).

In His initial call and commission to Ezekiel, God laid the burden of being a watchman for His people Israel upon him (see Eze. 3:17). Now in chapter 33 He is reiterating it.

Today God's call to Ezekiel comes to us as a people. But it comes with special poignancy to those who are or regard themselves as spiritual leaders. And the interesting thing is that God does not hold all, even among His true followers, equally responsible. There were other true followers of God among the Jews in Babylonian exile. Among these were Daniel and his companions at the Babylonian court: Shadrach, Meshach, and Abednego, and probably untold others. But these were not specifically called to be God's spokesmen. They were to live and witness for God.

The same was true in the time of Elijah. Elijah erroneously thought he alone was God's true servant during Ahab's widespread apostasy. But that was not the case. God told the despairing prophet that He had 7,000 loyal followers throughout the land of Israel (see 1 Kings 19:14, 18, NKJV). One of these true-blue ones was at Ahab's court—"Obadiah, who was in charge of [Ahab's] house. (Now Obadiah feared the Lord greatly)" (1 Kings 18:3, NKJV). While Jezebel was massacring God's prophets, Obadiah secreted 100 of them in caves and furnished them with food and water (verse 4).

As a watchman on the walls of the city was to alert its inhabitants of approaching enemies, so Ezekiel was to alert the exiles that if they did not return in obedience to God, they would all ultimately die without God and salvation. Noah had sounded God's warning to the antediluvians, but in vain. Only his own family went with him into the ark despite his 120 years of evangelism. Some may have heeded his warning and accepted salvation but died before the Flood came, as did Methuselah.

Apparently Ezekiel's warnings were not fruitless. His

pleas did reach the hearts of all and resulted in repentance of some and they said, "We are burdened with our sins and the wrongs we have done. We are wasting away. How can we live?" (Eze. 33:10, TEV).

God's answer through Ezekiel came back to the hearers: "Tell them that as surely as I, the Sovereign Lord, am the living God, I do not enjoy seeing a sinner die. I would rather see him stop sinning and live. Israel, stop the evil you are doing. Why do you want to die?" (verse 11, TEV). God assured them that there was forgiveness, and power to heal every contrite, sin-sick soul.

But Judah as a nation was stubbornly unrepentant. Destruction of Judah was inevitable. Jeremiah mourned with his colleague Ezekiel in Babylon. He expressed his lament of his nation's failure in this way: "The harvest is past, the summer is ended, and we are not saved" (Jer. 8:20).

Jeremiah was crushed by the utter ruin that awaited his people, and mourned: "For the wound of the daughter of my people is my heart wounded. I mourn, and dismay has taken hold of me" (verse 21).

"Was there no balm for Israel's spiritual wounds and no healer to apply it? The answer implied is, 'Yes, there is.' The message borne by the prophets, if heeded, would have provided healing" (*The SDA Bible Commentary*, vol. 4, p. 394). There was, and still is, balm in Gilead. The American Negro spiritual expresses it beautifully:

"There is a balm in Gilead to make the wounded whole;
There is a balm in Gilead to heal the sin-sick soul."

---

* There have been, and possibly still are, people who have lived under conditions that gave no opportunity to develop and use their God-intended freedom of choice. Those who have coerced and kept them in this state will be held responsible for their wrongdoing. "I saw that the slave master will have to answer for the soul of his slave whom he has kept in ignorance; and the sins of the slave will be visited upon the master" (Ellen G. White, *Early Writings*, p. 276).

C H A P T E R 8

THE FILTHY FOUNDLING

Based on Ezekiel 16; 20; and 23

Ezekiel's allegories in chapters 16 and 23 rehearse Israel's and Judah's sinful histories. Both nations willfully departed from God's known will and way. In chapter 16 this is illustrated by the story of the filthy foundling. In chapter 23 their perverseness is depicted by the unchaste lives of the two women Oholah and Oholibah, representing Israel and Judah. Chapter 20 is a historical recital of the same divergence from God's plan by these two nations.

This chapter rests mainly on the story of the filthy foundling in chapter 16. The other two are only occasionally referred to. These three chapters are variant portrayals of Israel's and Judah's grossness in sin.

In Ezekiel 16 God said to His prophet: "Son of man, make known to Jerusalem her abominations" (verse 2). Then follows the story of the filthy foundling. In a modern rendition it reads:

"When you were born, no one cared for you. When I first saw you, your umbilical cord was uncut, and you had been neither washed nor rubbed with salt nor clothed. No one had the slightest interest in you; no one pitied you or cared for you. On that day when you were born, you were dumped out into a field and left to die, unwanted.

"But I came by and saw you there, covered with your

56

own blood, and I said, 'Live! Thrive like a plant in the field!' And you did! You grew up and became tall, slender and supple, a jewel among jewels. And when you reached the age of maidenhood your breasts were full-formed and your pubic hair had grown; yet you were naked.

"Later, when I passed by and saw you again, you were old enough for marriage; and I wrapped my cloak around you to legally declare my marriage vow. I signed a covenant with you, and you became mine.

"Then, when the marriage had taken place, I gave you beautiful clothes of linens and silk, embroidered, and sandals made of dolphin hide. I gave you lovely ornaments, bracelets and beautiful necklaces, a ring for your nose and two more for your ears, and a lovely tiara for your head. And so you were made beautiful with gold and silver, and your clothes were silk and linen and beautifully embroidered. You ate the finest foods and became more beautiful than ever. You looked like a queen, and so you were! Your reputation was great among the nations for your beauty; it was perfect because of all the gifts I gave you, says the Lord God.

"But you thought you could get along without me—you trusted in your beauty instead; and gave yourself as a prostitute to every man who came along. Your beauty was his for the asking" (verses 4-15, TLB).

This allegory of the female foundling begins with the Israelites in Egyptian bondage. God took pity on her, and the nation of Israel was born.

After the girl reached maturity, God married her by entering into a covenant relationship with her at Sinai. Through this she became a queen (verse 13). The queen attained greatness and beauty among the nations because of the gifts God copiously gave her. This period of wealth and beauty represents Israel during the reigns of David and Solomon, when the kingdom of Israel stretched "from the Euphrates to the land of the Philistines and to the border of Egypt" (1 Kings 4:21).

Attaining this eminence in the community of nations led

God to remark reprovingly: "You thought you could get along without me—you trusted in your beauty instead" (Eze. 16: 15, TLB).

The queen's prostitution represents Israel's entering into alliances with foreign nations and her moral descent to worshiping their idols. Israel sank morally lower than the heathen nations around her. Figuratively Ezekiel expressed her moral decline this way: "Prostitutes charge for their services—men pay with many gifts. But not you, you give them gifts, bribing them to come to you! So you are different from other prostitutes. But you had to pay them, for no one wanted you" (verses 33, 34, TLB).

Israel not only lost her former renown and glory among the nations but sank so low morally that even her heathen neighbors "were ashamed" of her "lewd behavior" (verse 27).

In Egyptian bondage the Israelites had almost lost sight of God's law. The Sabbath had been generally disregarded, since the exactions of their taskmasters rendered its observance impossible. To remedy this failure, God gave the Ten Commandments to Moses in written form. These "were representative of God's love in that its injunctions, both negative and positive, led not to restriction of life, but to fullness of life. It demanded a response of love, not because obedience would somehow accumulate credit in the sight of God, but because the grace of God, experienced already in liberation from Egypt and in the divine initiative in the covenant promise, elicited such a response from man in gratitude" (P. C. Craigie, *The Book of Deuteronomy* [Grand Rapids: Eerdmans, 1976], p. 150).

But instead of keeping the seventh-day Sabbath as a sign, or flag—signaling that they were the Creator-God's representatives among the nations on earth (see Eze. 20:12, 20)—the Israelites began to "profane" or "pollute" (KJV) it. Instead of permitting it to be a sign of spiritual growth, or sanctification, they were irked by it and wanted it to pass quickly so they could resume their secular activities (see Amos 8:5, 6). The Sabbath became a burden to them rather than a delight, as

God had purposed (see Isa. 58:13). They did not observe it "with joyfulness and gladness of heart" (Deut. 28:47), as God wanted them to.

Israel's desire to reduce the Sabbath to the level of a common day left no barrier to idolatry. "The Sabbath, as a memorial of God's creative power, points to Him as the maker of the heavens and the earth. Hence it is a constant witness to His existence and a reminder of His greatness, His wisdom, and His love. Had the Sabbath always been sacredly observed, there could never have been an atheist or an idolater." "God's claim to reverence and worship, above the gods of the heathen, is based on the fact that He is the Creator, and that to Him all other beings owe their existence" (White, *Patriarchs and Prophets*, p. 336). The removal of the Creator-God from the awareness of the Israelites opened the floodgates to every other heathen perversion.

Israel experienced moral collapse before it lost its political power and ceased to exist as a nation. Its end came during the reign of the Assyrian king Shalmaneser in 722 B.C., probably through his general Sargon, who shortly succeeded him on the throne.

When Judah met its end in 586 B.C., it had sunk far lower than even Israel and the Sodomites (see Eze. 16:46-48). She, like Israel before her, had profaned the Sabbath and defiled the sanctuary (see Eze. 23:38).

At the Exodus God told the Israelites to build Him the sanctuary, later replaced by Solomon's resplendent Temple, as His symbolic dwelling place "in their midst" (Ex. 25:8). God Himself wanted their companionship; He wanted to fellowship with His people. But instead of the Temple becoming a venue for fellowship with God, Israel turned it into a place of idol worship (see Eze. 8).

And the purpose of the Sabbath was to afford the people one day in seven when they could lay aside the work and cares of life. This day they would devote time to personal fellowship with God by meditating upon His power and goodness. A vivid remembrance of God's blessings and mercy would awaken gratitude toward Him, not only as the giver of every good gift but, as the Creator. Remembering Him as the Creator of the physical world, they would learn to recognize Him also as their Re-Creator unto holiness and life eternal. God said that their keeping of the Sabbath was to be a sign and reminder to them "that I, the Lord, make them [you] holy" (Eze. 20:12, TEV). With their permission and personal cooperation God would transform them and make them holy.

Despite having observed the judgment that had befallen Israel because of her disregard of God's will, Judah did not hesitate to step even deeper into the mire of sin. She heeded no warnings. Under the symbol of Oholibah, Ezekiel said that "Oholibah [Judah] saw this, yet she was more corrupt than she [Israel] in her doting and in her harlotry, which was worse than that of her sister" (Eze. 23:11).

Israel's idolatry appears incredible after all that God had done for them. He took a group of slaves and made them a nation. He fought for His people in war. He rendered them immune to Balaam's sorcery. Their unity with God had been their shield. In obedience to His will they were stronger than armies. God had protected them from both armies, sorceries, and sickness, and made them into a strong and prosperous nation. Yet they turned away from Him to idols. God said: "During your disgusting life as a prostitute you never once remembered your childhood—when you were naked, squirming in your own blood" (Eze. 16:22, TEV).

What was God's purpose in reminding Judah of these terrible experiences from the past? Such dreadful memories.

Memories. Do they help or hinder? Do they break down one's courage, or do they give more skill and impart strength to cope more successfully with daily challenges?

All of us have memories of at least two broad categories. Some remind us of victories and successes of the past. Others are miserable and remind us of past failures and defeats. It may depend on a person's attitude whether memories hurt or help.

Memories of past successes, even amid difficulties, do strengthen and fortify us for the difficult tasks of today. We should erect mental memorials of these. God told His children of old to do this. After the Israelites crossed the

Jordan on their entry into the Promised Land, God told Joshua to make a cairn at Gilgal to memorialize their miraculous crossing (see Joshua 4). As their children would look at this heap of stones and ask about its purpose, their parents would tell them what God had done for their forefathers. Samuel built his Ebenezer (see 1 Sam. 7:12)—a memorial to God's help—after the defeat of the Philistines to enable Israel to remember what God had done for them. Our successes make us rejoice. They give us new courage and strength, even when tired, to continue along the path of God's will.

But what about miserable memories? All of us also have some of past failures and defeats. Israel-Judah had such galore. But why should Ezekiel, who in the end is a prophet of hope, remind his people of these unfortunate apostasies of the past?

Would the remembrance of all these past failures discourage the Jews, or help them? Do the memories of defeats discourage or help you and me?

Whether or not unfortunate past experiences discourage or help us to live more successfully today depends on a person's attitude toward them. God hoped that the Jews, and all His followers even today, would stop and think of their past failures. That they'd analyze them to try to ascertain why their course ended in defeat and failure. And that they should then extract all they could learn from their past mistakes in order not to repeat them. In such a way they would avoid falling into the same trap again.

Some people refuse to devote any thought to a mistake or defeat of the past. They hate the very mention of it, and emphatically let anyone know that by announcing, "Don't mention it." People who follow such a course have paid tuition in the school of life without reaping any reward from it. That is unfortunate.

As we analyze a suffered defeat, we should find out what contributed to or caused the failure. Then we should decide not to repeat what spelled failure rather than led to success. If this is a person's attitude, failures pave the way to success.

Edison, the world's greatest inventor, was never baffled

by failure. Before he succeeded in inventing the electric light, he failed innumerable times. And he experienced still more failures in trying to produce the storage battery. About 10,000 experiments failed to produce results. When a friend tried to console him about his repeated failures, Edison's response was "Why, I have not failed. I've just found 10,000 ways that won't work."

Edison learned from failure because he chose not to repeat in an identical way an experiment that resulted in failure. By discarding the ways he had found did not work and by incessantly trying new ways, Edison finally hit upon a way that produced light and led him to the invention of the storage battery. Not having the benefit of anyone who had blazed the inventive trail before him in these areas, Edison had to forge his own way. Defining genius as "1 percent inspiration and 99 percent perspiration," he reaped success through persistence. By sticking to these principles, Edison achieved the impossible.

God wished that Judah would choose to learn from their past failures by refusing to pursue a course that already had spelled defeat. But they did not. Hence failure dogged them until their nation ceased to exist. The Jews had an advantage over Edison in his inventive work. God had explicitly told them what would not bring peace and happiness and success in life. In Deuteronomy 28 Moses, their first leader, under inspiration from God had outlined for them what would bring success. He had also foretold what would bring failure and ultimate disaster and curses upon them.

After we, as children of God, have asked Him to forgive us for our past mistakes, we should not rue over them. But it is wise to analyze them and extract all we can learn from them before we consign them to oblivion.

When Satan reminds us of our failures in order to discourage us, we should promptly inform him that although we did indeed fail, those defeats have been blotted out by the shed blood of Jesus. We should quote to him God's unfailing promise as stated by the apostle John in 1

John 1:9: "If we confess our sins, he is faithful and just to forgive us our sins, and to cleanse us from all unrighteousness" (KJV).

God reminded His children through the prophet Ezekiel of their past stumblings, so that they would not fall into the same pit again. He envisioned a better and more successful future for restored Israel, since "memories are the key not to the past, but to the future," as John and Elizabeth Sherrill have observed in *The Hiding Place* (Chosen Books).

CHAPTER 9

THE ULTIMATE RULER
OF THE NATIONS

Based on Ezekiel 25-32

Many a Christian tends to limit God's concern and activity. He may think of Him as his God, his church's God, or the God of the Christian world. God, he is prone to think, exists to meet his needs, respond to his interests, and answer his prayers. In this way he may privatize God and almost consider Him his own patron saint.

The Hebrew prophets had no such insular views of God. They were true monotheists. To the Hebrew prophets, in contradistinction to the thinking of many a Jew, their God was the only true God and the Creator of heaven and earth. They thought of the earth's Creator as being concerned and caring for the whole human family, both Jew and Gentile. Believing in the Creator-God, they looked upon Him as having the whole world in His hands—as the ultimate ruler of all nations.

In keeping with His rulership of all the earth, God had hoped that all nations and every individual would seek Him and serve Him. The apostle Paul presented this concept to the Athenians on Mars' Hill by saying that God "made every nation of men" "so that men would seek him and perhaps reach out for him and find him" (Acts 17:26, 27, NIV). It was—and is—possible for every person to find God, provided his attitude was—and is—one of willingly seeking for

God. The prophet Isaiah, in speaking for God, said: "I revealed myself to those who did not ask for me; I was found by those who did not seek me" (Isa. 65:1, NIV).

Paul in Romans 1:19, 20 elaborates on God's revelation to the Gentiles. Even though they did not know God as did the Israelites, who had been "entrusted with the oracles of God" (Rom. 3:2), they were without excuse. They possessed His book of nature. About this Paul wrote: "For what can be known about God is plain to them, because God has shown it to them. Ever since the creation of the world his invisible nature, namely, his eternal power and deity, has been clearly perceived in the things that have been made. So they are without excuse" (Rom. 1:19, 20).

The psalmist affirms that through the book of nature God speaks to everyone. "There is no speech or language where their voice [referring to the heavens in verse 1] is not heard. Their voice goes out into all the earth, their words to the ends of the world" (Ps. 19:3, 4, NIV). The very heavens speak of the creatorship of God and His might and glory. Their speech never ceases. "Day after day they pour forth speech" (verse 2, NIV). This proclamation of God is perpetual. Neither a preacher nor a book can impress a human mind equally continuously.

Besides the book of nature, the Holy Spirit speaks to each person. He is the representative of Jesus, who is "the real light—the light that comes into the world and shines on all mankind" (John 1:9, TEV). The Spirit works through the conscience. As the instrument of the Holy Spirit, the conscience does not tell us what is right. That is the office of the Word of God (see Ps. 119:105; Prov. 6:23). But the conscience tells each person to do what he knows or thinks is right.

Paul further indicates that the Gentiles, if true to their inmost self, would know to do right: "(Indeed, when Gentiles, who do not have the law, do by nature things required by the law, they are a law for themselves, even though they do not have the law, since they show that the requirements of the law are written on their hearts, their consciences also bearing witness and their thoughts now accusing, now even defending them)" (Rom. 2:14, 15, NIV).

"As through Christ every human being has life, so also through Him every soul receives some ray of divine light. Not only intellectual but spiritual power, a perception of right, a desire for goodness, exists in every heart" (White, *Education*, p. 29). Paul, in speaking to the Gentiles at Lystra, referred to God's goodness by saying that God "has not left you without some clue to his nature, in the kindness he shows" (Acts 14:17, NEB).

It was only after His plan of speaking personally and directly to each person proved unworkable that God chose Abraham to raise up a nation to be His special representatives in the world. "The Lord finally left the hardened transgressors to follow their evil ways, while He chose Abraham . . . and made him the keeper of His law for future generations" (White, *Patriarchs and Prophets*, p. 125).

In this way God's primary concern in Old Testament times became the Israelites. The apostle Paul referred to this when he said: "In past generations he [God] allowed all the nations [Gentiles] to walk in their own ways" (Acts 14:16). From among all nations God had chosen the Israelites and set them apart to be lights in the world. They, hopefully, were to direct the attention of those with whom they came in contact to their God—the only true God.

Both the nation as a whole and the Israelites as individuals were to be witnesses for God. Rahab, the harlot in Jericho, accepted the God of Israel as her God after seeing what God had done for them as a nation (see Joshua 2:9-24). Through the Israelites God's name was to "be declared throughout all the earth" (Ex. 9:16), and they were to be a blessing to the nations. "God's covenant with him [Abraham] embraced all nations of earth" (Ellen G. White, *Prophets and Kings*, p. 368).

Individual Israelites did bring God's saving grace to Gentiles. Ruth the Moabitess had turned to the true God through the influence of Naomi, her mother-in-law (see Ruth 1:14-17). The little Israelite slave girl in Naaman's household in Syria was instrumental in leading Naaman, the commander of the army of the king of Syria, to have faith in the God of Israel (see 2 Kings 5:17-19).

Ideally, Israel should always have advertised God favorably, as it did during the early years of Solomon's reign. "King Solomon excelled all the kings of the earth in riches and wisdom. And the whole earth sought the presence of Solomon to hear his wisdom, which God had put into his mind" (1 Kings 10:23, 24). One of the seekers from afar was the queen of Sheba (see verses 6-10). She recognized that God had favored Solomon with wisdom. Loyalty to God and His commandments brought honor to Israel among the nations, as was God's intention (see Deut. 4:6).

But as Solomon lapsed in his commitment to God, so did other rulers and the nation. Instead of being witnesses to God's saving power and transmitting moral virtue and wisdom to the heathen, the Israelites sank deep into the mire of sin. The prophets tried to stem this bent toward evil, but in vain. "Had Israel been true to her trust, all the nations of earth would have shared in her blessings. But the hearts of those to whom had been entrusted a knowledge of saving truth were untouched by the needs of those around them. As God's purpose was lost sight of, the heathen came to be looked upon as beyond the pale of His mercy. The light of truth was withheld, and darkness prevailed. The nations were overspread with a veil of ignorance; the love of God was little known; error and superstition flourished" *(ibid.,* p. 371).

Israel, who was designed to model God's character of love, truth, and undeviating loyalty to the Creator-God, failed. Instead the Israelites became trailblazers in wickedness. They rebelled against God's "ordinances more than the nations," and against His "statutes more than the countries round about her" (Eze. 5:6). They became leaders, not in guiding the heathen to learn to know God, but in departure from God's will. The pagan Philistines were ashamed of Israel's "lewd behavior" (Eze. 16:27). Even Israel, God's chosen people, helped frustrate God's intention for the nations.

God unveiled the true object of national government to Nebuchadnezzar, king of Babylon, "under the figure of a great tree, whose height 'reached unto heaven, and the sight thereof to the end of all the earth: the leaves thereof were fair, and the fruit thereof much, and it was meat for all'; under its shadow the beasts of the field dwelt, and among its branches the birds of the air had their habitation (Dan. 4:11, 12, KJV). This representation shows the character of a government that fulfills God's purpose—a government that protects and upbuilds the nation.

"God exalted Babylon that it might fulfill this purpose. Prosperity attended the nation until it reached a height of wealth and power that has never since been equaled—fitly represented in the Scriptures by the inspired symbol, a 'head of gold' (Dan. 2:38, KJV)" (White, *Education,* p. 175). Through the prophet Isaiah God called "Babylon, that pearl of kingdoms, the jewel and boast of Chaldaeans" (Isa. 13:19, Jerusalem).

Prosperity and ill fortune among nations are not matters of divine caprice. Both result from a nation's compliance or violation of God's purpose for it. "Each [nation] had its period of test, each failed, its glory faded, its power departed, and its place was occupied by another" *(ibid.,* p. 177).

But God does not measure sin and guilt as men do. God measures a nation's—and a person's—wrongdoing against the amount of divine light the nation or person possesses. In this way a nation can be grossly sinful in men's eyes but be rather innocent in the eyes of God. The prophet Habakkuk illustrates this.

At about the time Josiah began to reign (c. 640 B.C.). Habakkuk cried to God about the rampant wickedness in Israel. He wondered why God did not do something to stop it. He told God: "The law is slacked and justice never goes forth" (Hab. 1:4).

In answer to Habakkuk's quandary God told him that the Chaldeans, or Babylonians, would soon come to punish Israel (see verses 5-11). This intensified the prophet's perplexity rather than alleviated it, since the Babylonians were more wicked than the Jews (see verse 13). To Habakkuk it was incomprehensible that God would permit the bloody Babylonians to punish Judah. In the eyes of the Jews, including the prophet Habakkuk, the Babylonians were more sinful than they were. But the Jews, with more knowledge of God's will than the Babylonians, had exhausted their period of test, while the Babylonians had not.

Ezekiel saw and recorded the fulfillment of Habakkuk's prophecy about Judah. Having done this, he goes on and shows that other nations also are subject to the inexorable laws of like returns. Each will reap what he sows.

Judgment prophecies on seven foreign nations, all neighbors that had been a thorn in the flesh of Judah, now follow in Ezekiel 25-32. God turned Ezekiel's attention to these foreign powers only after judgment had fallen on Judah. To the perceptive Jew this was a reminder that God is indeed the ruler of all nations. As God held Israel responsible for its sins, so He also holds other nations accountable for their deeds. Starting with the Ammonites to the northeast of Judah, Ezekiel proceeds in circle fashion toward the south, west, and north, ending with Sidon on the Mediterranean coast. Then he jumps further southwest, ending with Egypt.

The Ammonites lived in what is now part of the kingdom of Jordan. They were blood relatives of the Israelites by being the descendants of Lot by his younger daughter (see Gen. 19:38). Despite the common origin, Ammonite history is one of merciless cruelty toward the Israelites. In the day of their political power they perpetrated the traditional cruelty to the Israelites—ripping open pregnant women in Gilead (see Amos 1:13).

Despite Ammonite hatefulness, the Israelites nevertheless copied their Molech worship by having their sons and daughters pass through fire, contrary to God's expressed command (see Lev. 18:21; 20:3-5; 2 Kings 23:10; Jer. 32:35). At Jerusalem's fall to Nebuchadnezzar in 586 B.C. the Ammonites expressed their gleeful animosity by clapping their hands in rejoicing (see Eze. 25:3, 6).

The Ammonites learned nothing from the calamity that overtook Judah. They were blind. As a consequence God declared the Ammonites would be utterly destroyed as a nation and their capital, Rabbah, razed (see Eze. 25:7). They would reap what they had sown. So would the nations of Moab, Edom, and Philistia, on which Ezekiel pronounced judgment in rapid succession.

The Moabites were brothers or cousins of the Ammonites by their father Lot and an older sister to the mother of Ammon (see Gen. 19:36, 37).

The sin of the Moabites (Eze. 25:8-11) seems to have been that they looked upon Judah as any other nation. They assumed that God had been unable to protect the Jews and Jerusalem from the Babylonians. The God of the Hebrews, they reasoned, was just as helpless as their gods. Such thinking degraded God.

The Edomites (verses 12-14) were descendants of Esau, Jacob's brother. They lived south of the Moabites. Their judgment in this chapter should be coupled with chapter 35, directed to Seir, another name for Edom. The Edomites had cherished perpetual enmity toward Jacob's descendants, the Israelites, since Esau sold his birthright to Jacob (see Gen. 25:29-34; 27:18-29, 41). This hatred reappeared at the Exodus when Edom refused to let Israel pass through its territory (see Num. 20:14-21). This animosity manifested itself at the Babylonian siege of Jerusalem. The Edomites assisted the Babylonians by preventing the escape of Jewish fugitives (see Obadiah 14-21).

All these nations had rejoiced at the political misfortunes of God's people. When Jerusalem faced total destruction before the army of Nebuchadnezzar, the Edomites joyously exclaimed, "Rase it, rase it! Down to its foundations!" (Ps. 137:7). They manifested the spirit of Satan. God, on the other hand, as shown by Jesus, is filled with grief when His earth children suffer by reaping the results of their departure from His will (Matt. 23:37, 38).

Among the prophecies against the nations Ezekiel devotes much time to the Phoenician kingdom and particularly its great merchant city Tyre (Eze. 26-28:19). The charge against Tyre was its joy at the fall of Jerusalem and Judah (see Eze. 26:1, 8). Through their destruction a commercial competitor for coveted trade would be eliminated.

Ezekiel's picture of Tyre's destruction is an antitype of the fall of spiritual Babylon portrayed in Revelation 17 and 18. Its king is a symbol of Satan and his degradation ending with total loss of power and utter ruin. The revelator's portrayal of the downfall of the great harlot Babylon brings the phrases penned by the prophet Ezekiel about the overthrow of historical Tyre to one's mind. Many of John's thoughts and expressions parallel Ezekiel's.*

No specific offense is listed in the prophecy against Sidon. But when God would manifest His glory Sidonians would recognize that the God of Israel is the true Lord.

Ezekiel directs his last and longest prophecy against Egypt (Eze. 29-32). One of its sins was its halfhearted response to Zedekiah's appeal for help during the Babylonian siege of Jerusalem (see Eze. 29; cf. Jer. 37:7). But its gravest fault was pride.

In poetic language God likened Egypt in its greatness to a mighty cedar of Lebanon with its top in the clouds, rivaling the trees in God's own garden in beauty (see Eze. 3:1, 3, 8, 9). Because of its greatness, Egypt swelled with pride (see Eze. 29:9, 10). Pharaoh Hophra, also called Apries, boasted that "not even a god could dispossess him of his power" (*The SDA Bible Commentary*, vol. 4, p. 678).

There is no sin in greatness or strength. Craigie notes that "greatness is neither something to be ashamed of, nor something to be proud of. If it leads to pride, both in the form of self-conceit and the despising of others, then greatness cannot be retained. For true greatness, whether in the local or international aspects of human living, can only grow on humility and respect for others" (*Ezekiel*, p. 225).

As a result of its pride God's punishment would fall upon Egypt through the king of Babylon (see Eze. 30:8, 25). "For he [Pharaoh or Egypt] spread terror in the land of the living; therefore he shall be laid among those who are slain by the sword, Pharaoh and all his multitude, says the Lord God" (Eze. 32:32). Egypt had failed in its stewardship under God.

Among all these prophecies of condemnation on the surrounding nations there is no oracle against Babylon. During the time of Ezekiel's prophetic ministry Babylon was God's "battle axe and weapons of war" (Jer. 51:20, KJV), as Assyria had been the rod of God's anger, the staff of His fury (see Isa. 10:15) a century earlier. Babylon's time had not yet come. Its period of test had not yet run out. But it would surely come, as Jeremiah pointed out in chapters 51 and 52. Daniel was still in Babylon the night the fatal blow fell (see Dan. 5).

At the Exodus God gave the land of Canaan to the Israelites, not because of their righteousness, but because of the wickedness of its former inhabitants. Moses cautioned them: "Do not say in your heart, after the Lord your God has thrust them out before you, 'It is because of my righteousness that the Lord has brought me in to possess this land'; whereas it is because of the wickedness of these nations that the Lord is driving them out before you. . . . Know therefore, that the Lord your God is not giving you this good land to possess because of your righteousness; for you are a stubborn people" (Deut. 9:4-6).

At the time of the Exodus the Canaanite nations had exhausted their period of test. And so they were driven out because they had filled their measure of wickedness. This had not been the case in the days of Abraham. Then God had said: "The sin of the Amorites has not yet reached its full measure" (Gen. 15:16, NIV). During the reign of Zedekiah Israel had reached its full measure of wickedness, and passed off its stage of history. Babylon's doom was still in the future.

Naturally Babylon did not possess the same knowledge and insight into God's will that the Israelites did. But God held the Babylonians responsible for loyalty to the knowledge they did possess.

Most of these nations upon which Ezekiel pronounced God's judgment were to be destroyed and disappear. Israel, although destroyed, was to reappear and grow strong and prosperous.

From the ruins of these heathen nations, God would gather a remnant to join restored Israel. So He will also glean a remnant from all nations for His eternal kingdom. Individuals would—and will—forsake their idolatrous practices and join themselves to Israel.

---

* Compare Ezekiel 26-28 with Revelation 17 and 18. See also *The SDA Bible Commentary,* vol. 4, pp. 668, 669.

CHAPTER 10

SHEPHERDS, SHEEP, AND SALVATION

Based on Ezekiel 34

In chapter 34 God turns Ezekiel's thoughts, not primarily to the people, but to the rulers of Israel under the symbol of "the shepherds of Israel" (verse 2). During the short reign of Jehoichin, Jeremiah gave a prophecy that parallels Ezekiel's (see Jer. 23:1-8).

Rulers are often designated shepherds in the Bible. Through the prophet Isaiah, God called the Persian king Cyrus His shepherd (see Isa. 44:28). Spiritual leaders were also called shepherds. Moses and David, who had both herded sheep, called themselves shepherds, as leaders of God's people (see Isa. 63:11; Ps. 78:70). In this chapter God speaks of both civil and spiritual leaders as shepherds.

To acquaint myself with a shepherd's life and responsibilities, I accompanied (by way of reading) the Basque herder Rosalio as he took his herd of more than 1,500 sheep on a 52-day spring trek of 200 miles from around Phoenix, Arizona, to cool summer pastures above 8,000 feet, close to the New Mexico border. On this trip Rosalio was the sole herder, assisted by a few dogs and some goats.

Goats are needed as leaders. They help the shepherds find the best feeding grounds. There are also many places where the sheep refuse to go except as followers. From my childhood in Sweden I distinctly remember the difference in attitude and behavior between our goats and sheep. Goats are active, daring, adventurous, and unafraid. Sheep appear placid, timid, and helpless. After they had been holed up in the barn the whole winter, it was interesting to observe their reaction to freedom when they were let loose outdoors in the spring. The sheep walked out sedately, leisurely. The goats, on the other hand, scampered around, climbing any and every rock curiously and unafraid, venturing out on any high and narrow ledge. For this reason sheepherders use goats as leaders. With a goat leading the way, the sheep are willing and ready to follow.

On this long trek Rosalio's tasks were manifold. He had to protect his wards against marauding coyotes, mountain lions, and even bears. For him there was no rest, not even on a rainy day. Even then his herd needed fresh pasture. And it was not always plentiful in the desert, where the sheep at times had to go for more than 70 hours without water. It was Roaslio's job to find and lead his sheep to both pasture and watering places.

In addition to being their protector and provider, he was their physician. He nursed the sick, helped the lame, and even carried the weak across the difficult places.

His ears were constantly alert to the sheep's bleating. Amid their cries of "Baa! Baa!" Rosalio could discern a sheep's plea for help. One day a sheep was stranded in rocks, and he went to help it. To do so, he took off his shoes to descend a perilous, slippery rock to a ledge, where a silly, self-trapped ewe stood bleating. Another day Rosalio detected the cry of a lamb in distress. He found it wedged between two rocks. If he had not responded to its call for help, those rocks would have been its tombstones.

He kept constant check of all his charges. One day they spread out into four ravines. He did not trust his dogs to round up all the sheep, so he himself scoured each ravine, looking behind each bush and boulder. On this trek he consequently walked a distance perhaps four times longer than his sheep.

Every few days he would take a census to make sure all

his sheep were still with him. If the count was not right he would untiringly go in search of his lost sheep until he found it.

Rosalio lived for his sheep. He never permitted weariness to prevail over compassion, and no act of mercy to his sheep was too onerous for him. Because of this single-minded commitment to the care of his sheep, Rosalio arrived at the summer pastures without the loss of one (adapted from Francis R. Line, "Arizona Sheep Trek," *National Geographic* 97, No. 4 [April 1950]: 457-478).

The leaders of Israel, on the other hand, did not live to serve their people as a herder does his sheep. They were self-seeking and self-caring. They fed themselves, not their sheep. They ate their fat and dressed in their wool (see Eze. 34:2, 3). They did not care for the sick or help the weak, as did Rosalio. Nor did they seek those who had strayed. They certainly did not carry the weak. Rather, they ruled their sheep with hardness (see verse 4).

The last shepherds of Israel, with the four successors of Josiah on the throne, were constantly looking out for their own interests and good. They pauperized the people by taking their possessions and wealth—"their fat"—through exorbitant taxes. "They were like parasites in the fleeces of their flock, not leaders and guardians of their people" (Craigie, *Ezekiel*, p. 242).

Compared to the Basque herder, the shepherds of Israel were no shepherds at all. They failed to guide the flock in safe paths. In this way they weakened the people and prepared the nation for its demise. And the majority of the Israelites forgot their commitment to the God of their fathers and followed their evildoing shepherds into sinful forgetfulness of the God of Israel and brought Israel rapidly to the end of its probationary time.

They were shepherds like the Reverend Jim Jones of Jonestown, Guyana, notoriety. Jones was born in Indiana in 1931. His mother was convinced he was a messiah. Jim came to share her convictions. Without any formal theological training he began serving as a minister in his early 20s. In 1956 he started his People's Temple in Indianapolis.

The People's Temple centered its belief not in God, but in "Dad," a title Jones adopted early in his ministry. The basic tenet was total allegiance and obedience to Jones himself. Physical beatings were administered to those who challenged his authority.

In 1965 Jones moved his People's Temple to California, where he enlarged his ministry to include sham miracle healings. He took mistresses from among his Temple members. Exposure of Jones' corruption, sadism, sexual acts, and drug dependency caused Jones and his Temple members to leave hastily for Guyana in 1976.

In Guyana, Jones and his nearly 1,000 followers lived in an agricultural settlement out of public view until November 18, 1978. On that day more than 900 people followed him to death by drinking from a vat of soft drink laced with cyanide. This was precipitated by the coming of California congressman Leo. J. Ryan to investigate rumors that several of the cult members were being held against their will. At this Jones told his followers that "everyone has to die. If you love me as I love you, we must all die or be destroyed from the outside." To accomplish this, the cultists had to take the fatal drink (see Richard C. Schroeder, "Jonestown," *Encyclopedia Americana*, 1989 ed.).

This sounds dreadful. But just as surely as Jones led his followers to death, so did the shepherds of Israel in the days of Ezekiel. Zedekiah and his fellow leaders caused the destruction of Jerusalem. In the fearful carnage that ensued, not 900 but untold thousands died, in addition to those who died from famine before its fall.

Since Israel's shepherds had neglected their responsibility to their subjects, God said: "Behold, I, I myself will search for my sheep, and will seek them out" (verse 11). Although the Israelites were scattered because of a lack of true shepherds' care, God Himself would gather them from the nations and give them security again "upon the mountain heights" of Israel (verse 14).

Sheep are not looked upon as being intelligent animals. Rather, they are regarded as simple or just dumb. Goats are apparently much more intelligent and astute. Nevertheless,

God calls His followers sheep. To His 12 apostles Jesus said: "Behold, I send you out as sheep in the midst of wolves" (Matt. 10:16). And it is sheep, not goats, that are to be heirs of His kingdom (see Matt. 25:31-34), despite the goats' superior intelligence and evident leadership ability.

Sheep are by nature not leaders. They are followers. That is the reason sheepherders use goats as leaders for their sheep. God Himself made sheep that way. God's children are also made to be followers—followers of Jesus and followers of God's will as expressed in His Word; followers of the Holy Spirit, whom God desires to give to every receptive human being as a divine internal guide.

Throughout Scripture God repeatedly calls His followers sheep, and Jesus is the Good Shepherd (see John 10:1-18). When John the Baptist first introduced Jesus as the Redeemer he called Him "the Lamb of God" (John 1:29). The human Jesus was a sheep. Not independently running along His own path, but always willing to follow His Father's guidance and submit to His will.

Deep within, the human heart yearns for a good and true shepherd. Augustine said in his *Confessions*, "Thou hast made us for thyself, and our hearts are restless until they find rest in thee." And the only One who can adequately fill that need is Jesus. Only in Him can a person find lasting peace and security. Until he does find peace in Christ, he is constantly restless.

The Good Shepherd demonstrated heaven's interest in man. "Before the foundation of the world" (Eph. 1:4) He committed Himself to come to this earth to rescue His sheep if they would get caught in the enemy's clutches. In "the fulness of the time" (Gal. 4:4, KJV) He came as a man "to save the one lost sheep, the one world that [had] fallen by transgression" (White, *The Desire of Ages*, p. 693). As a true shepherd He did not rest satisfied with His myriads of unfallen worlds. He left the peace of heaven and entered the enemy's dominion to search for lost sheep. "For one sinner Christ would have laid down His life" (White, *Christ's Object Lessons*, p. 196).

As a true shepherd Jesus had—and has—compassion on

every human being in his weakness. He was not hard and condemnatory even on the weak and wicked. Like His Father He was "good to the ungrateful and the wicked" (Luke 6:35, TEV). "A bruised reed" He did not break, and "a smoldering wick" He did not snuff out (Isa. 42:3, NIV). "To the heart of Christ the very presence of trouble was a call for help. The poor, the sick, the desolate, the outcasts, the discouraged, the desponding, found in Him a compassionate Saviour, a mighty Healer" (Ellen G. White, *Medical Ministry*, p. 121). With solicitude He searched for all—even those who had strayed in sin like Mary, the sister of Lazarus and Martha; Matthew, the tax collector; and even scheming Judas, who finally betrayed Him. No one was excluded from His interest and care. Jesus had—and has—a good plan for each human being. To make this plan possible, He finally gave His life on Calvary.

Irrespective of how we respond to God's overtures of love, Jesus patiently and lovingly attempts to shepherd even His ungrateful and rebellious sheep to safe paths. He exhausts every means at His disposal to restore and save His sheep. He gave His life to rescue His sheep. When His love is unrequited, He weeps over their ultimate eternal death, as He did over Jerusalem (see Matt. 23:37).

As real sheep need herders, so do God's followers at all times need faithful leaders. The well-being of God's people, Israel—yes, their very existence—depended on shepherds who would lead them into an observance of their covenant relationship with God. But under unfaithful shepherds, like King Zedekiah and others before him, they disregarded the covenant and went their own way—the way to both personal and national ruin and destruction.

Peter had been a fisherman. He was following that vocation when Jesus called him and asked him to be a fisher of men. But in his Epistles Peter never refers to fishing. Rather, he speaks about shepherds. And Peter's charge to his fellow believers was to feed the flock, as Jesus Himself had told him to do (see John 21:15-17).

Sheepherding is a nobler vocation than fishing. Whatever the fisherman catches is caught to die. The shepherd is to care for sheep. His job is to see that his sheep are protected from danger, tenderly cared for when they are weak and sick, well fed and watered so that they may keep well and healthy and that the young ones may grow under his constantly watchful eye.

Years ago there lived in the Scottish Highlands a shepherd and his wife. His wife was about to deliver their first child. The shepherd had hoped it would be a boy to accompany him in his care for the sheep.

But it was a girl. And the father said: "Well, Mother, I will take her for my boy and make her a shepherd." And that's what he did. From her tender years of girlhood she was her father's constant companion. She knew the sheep as well as her father did. And she could give the shepherd's call as well as her father. The years went by. She reached late adolescence, and the father felt he could claim her no longer. He talked it over with his wife, and they decided their daughter should go to the great city of Glasgow. She was to be educated and become a real lady. At first she wrote her parents every day. Then once a week. Then only sporadically. Finally no letters came from her.

This was a blow to the parents. They were greatly troubled. They tried to find her, but to no avail. One day one of the boys from the village told the parents he had seen her in the city and went up to talk to her. But she rebuffed him. Evidently she wanted nothing to do with her old life.

Hearing this news, her parents were brokenhearted. Had they lost their girl? What could they do? At last the father said, "Mother, if she is alive, I'm going to find her."

"But you are not a city man," she said. "What can an old Highland shepherd like you do in the big city?"

The father knew he was not a city man. He was a shepherd. As a shepherd, he recalled that many a sheep had strayed. But every time one had strayed and seemed to be lost, he had searched for it until he found it. And so he told his wife, "I am going to Glasgow to find our daughter."

The father went, driven by the power of love. In the big city he found everything strange. And appearing as he did in his shepherd's cloak, he made an odd figure. The police were unable to give him any help. Nobody seemed to have any clue as to where his girl might be. For days he searched, but with no trace of her. At last he said to himself: "She knows the shepherd's call, and if she hears it, she will know I've come."

So early the next morning he began to go up and down the streets of the city where someone had hinted she might perchance be. He called and called, but got no reply. People looked out of the windows, wondering who such an odd fellow could be and why he was not arrested. All day long he called. Night was approaching. He was tired and grief-stricken. But still he kept on sounding his shepherd's call. He must find his girl.

In a house along a street where her shepherd father came calling sat a young woman surrounded by a group of friends. They were playing cards while drinking liquor and having a lively time. Hearing the call, she stopped and listened. "What's the matter?" one of them asked, looking at her in surprise.

"Listen!" she said. "Can you hear that? That's my father calling."

"Your dad! What do you mean? Come on, sit down. Let's go on with the game."

"No! I can't," she stammered. "I must go. That's my father calling." And flinging down her cards, she rushed to the door and down the street.

"Dad! Dad!" she cried. "You've come! You've come to find me." And she threw herself into his arms, weeping out her confession.

Yes, the old shepherd had come. He had sought and found his straying girl. In doing so, he had defied both custom and prestige. He had been searching for his lost one, and she had heard his shepherd's call and come.

That story shows the spirit of the true shepherd. He will not give up until he has found the lost sheep (adapted from Roy Allan Anderson, *The Shepherd-Evangelist* [Washington, D.C.: Review and Herald Pub. Assn., 1950], pp. 611-613).

Imagine what would happen if all of us undershepherds would care as unwearily for the sheep in our churches as did the Basque shepherd Rosalio, and seek the straying as untiringly as did the Scottish Highland shepherd his daughter. What if we were willing to die for the rescue of the sheep, if need be—as did the Good Shepherd? And heed the call of "the chief Shepherd" (1 Peter 5:4) with Spirit-guided zeal, as He admonishes, "Feed my lambs," "Tend my sheep," "Feed my sheep" (John 21:15-17)? What would the now-empty pews in our churches then look like?

CHAPTER 11

HEAVEN'S HEART SURGERY

Based on Ezekiel 11:17-21; 15; 36:16-38

It was God Himself who gave the Promised Land to the Israelites. This was a fulfillment of His repeated promise to Abraham (see Gen. 12:7; 13:14; 17:8). He placed them in a land flowing with milk and honey.

Canaan was a God-irrigated land. Not a land like Egypt, which had to be watered by its owners working the irrigation machinery by their feet (see Lev. 26:3, 4; cf. Deut. 11:10). So long as His people were true to God they did not need to worry about a suitable climate with ideal moisture to raise their crops (see 1 Kings 8:35). The children of Israel were to be like a treasured vineyard (see Isa. 5:7).

In parabolic language God said about Israel:
"My loved one had a vineyard
  On a fertile hillside.
 He dug it up and cleared it of stones
  And planted it with the choicest vines.
 He built a watchtower in it
  And cut out a winepress as well.
 Then he looked for a crop of good grapes,
  But it yielded only bad fruit" (verses 1, 2, NIV).

Palestine—the Promised Land—was the fertile hillside on which God planted His people when He brought them out of Egypt and made them a nation. It was God's original plan to remove its inhabitants from before them as a settler clears his field of stones. But His plan for removing Canaan's inhabitants from before the Israelites rested on their covenant relationship with Him.

God began His conquest of Canaan for them by giving them the city of Jericho. He Himself planned to fight their battles and prepare room for Israel, His choicest vine. Not faultless, but more ready than any other contemporary nation to follow His biddings. In Isaiah's parable the watchtower represented the Temple. The wall or hedge surrounding the vineyard symbolized His law.

"They were hedged about by the precepts of His law, the everlasting principles of truth, justice, and purity. Obedience to these principles was to be their protection, for it would save them from destroying themselves by sinful practices. And as the tower in the vineyard, God placed in the midst of the land His holy temple" (White, *Christ's Object Lessons*, pp. 287, 288).

The sole purpose of a vineyard is to produce good grapes. The wood from many trees is valuable for its choice lumber. But the wood of the vine is utterly useless for any purpose even when it is fresh and sound. If the vine does not bear grapes, it is good for nothing. It is not even desirable fuel; it is too crooked, small, and gnarled. In countries where other wood is available for fuel, the wood from the vine is burned as rubbish. Ezekiel in chapter 15 under the symbol of the vine pointed out Judah's purpose: to serve God loyally. Apart from this it was utterly worthless and fit only for destruction in fire.

Instead of producing fruit to the glory of God, Israel bore bad fruit (see Isa. 5:2). The bad fruit represented the abominations and detestable things Israel engaged in, like idol worship, etc. They even descended to the abominations of the surrounding heathen nations by sacrificing their children, having them go through fire to the Ammonite god Molech (see Jer. 32:35).

But God still loved His erring children. Although they were scattered among the nations, He still remembered them with solicitude and love. In His parable of the lost coin, the lost sheep, and the wayward son, Jesus in Luke 15 gave us a picture of His concern for all His children, even in the path of sin. As the sorrowing mother and father thought of their straying son in the far country among prostitutes and gamblers, so God in love thinks of His every earthborn child with concern. He has written the name of each on the palms of His hands (see Isa. 49:16). They are always on His mind. Jesus knows us individually, and is touched with the feeling of our infirmities. "He knows us all by name. He knows the very house in which we live, the name of each occupant" (White, *The Desire of Ages*, p. 479).

It would have been easy for God just to blot out the rebels on this earth and start anew. He could have created a new Adam and a new Eve after renovating this sin-contaminated globe in space. But He chose not to do so. For God loved Adam and Eve, and their prospective descendants, so that He gave His only-begotten Son for their redemption.

Our heavenly Father, in His unspeakable love for sinners, let Jesus leave the courts of glory and go in search for sinners. In doing so, He depleted the resources of heaven and emptied the storehouse on high. In heaven Jesus had been the adored, the leader of the heavenly host. But in coming to this earth He veiled His glory and became a man so that He could mingle and empathize with man. He humbled Himself to the lowest level of Jewish society. He was poor, formally uneducated, without position or reputation. He did this because He wanted to reach us and rescue us from our pit of sin. What God did for the world at large He did specifically for the Israelites. They had grievously gone against His will. They were scattered among the nations because of their sins. But He gave them another chance. He would gather them from their dispersion among the nations and bring them back to their own country. He, with their permission and cooperation, would free them from their addiction to wrongdoing—remove "all its detestable things and all its abominations" (Eze. 11:18) from their midst and country. Then He would give them a new heart.

For most of us it is pleasant to receive gifts. But not all good gifts are necessarily accepted, appreciated, and used. A letter is a gift. But not all letters are received with appreciation. In days when telephone conversations were not so common as today, a young woman received letters from a male friend. But she was angry with him, and so she never opened and read his letters. She spurned his overtures of love and attempts to restore the cordial relationship that had once existed between them. So God aimed to restore the cordial relationship that had once existed between Him and Israel, about which He said: "I remember the devotion of your youth, your love as a bride, how you followed me in the wilderness, in a land not sown. Israel was holy to the Lord" (Jer. 2:2, 3).

But such a friendship could be achieved only by the returning Israelites' willingness to receive a new heart.* Through such a change a person becomes "a new creation" (2 Cor. 5:17), or a "new being" (TEV). God's open promise to the Israelites was: "A new heart I will give you, and a new spirit I will put within you; and I will take out of your flesh the heart of stone and give you a heart of flesh. And I will put my spirit within you, and cause you to walk in my statutes and be careful to observe my ordinances" (Eze. 36:26, 27).

The "heart of stone" describes a state of spiritual insensitivity and moral indifference (see verse 26). This attitude God was willing to remove and to replace with one enabling them to "serve the Lord your God with joyfulness and gladness of heart" (Deut. 28:47). No longer would the Israelites be shackled by coerced obedience; instead they would be "willing and obedient" (Isa. 1:19) in relation to God's will. This was the attitude David hoped that Solomon would always sustain in his relationship with God by serving "him with a whole heart and with a willing mind" (1 Chron. 28:9).

In our times some surgical patients have received new hearts. But even in this age of heart transplants no one will receive a new physical heart through transplant surgery without his opting for such surgery. So no one will receive a new spiritual heart without a personal choice. A person who refuses to receive a new physical heart through transplant surgery may soon die. Those who refuse to receive the God-given new heart will ultimately die an eternal death.

The Israelites of old had refused to accept such a heart of flesh. They had cuddled their hearts of stone. This had led them to conflict with God's will. Finally, this rebelliousness ended not only in spiritual disaster but also in personal and national bankruptcy. It landed the Israelites in Assyrian captivity. And now it had landed Judah in Babylonian captivity. But God was not willing to give up on His people. He was determined to help them try again to live according to His will. If they were willing and prepared to receive a "new heart" and a "new spirit," glorious vistas would open up before them both as individuals and as a nation.

But the Jews of old were not the only ones who needed new hearts. Many of us today need new hearts. Our church is constantly growing. About this inspiration says: "Joining the church is one thing, and connecting with Christ is quite another. Not all the names registered in the church books are registered in the Lamb's book of life. Many, though apparently sincere believers, do not keep up a living connection with Christ. They have enlisted, they have entered their names on the register; but the inner work of grace is not wrought in the heart. As the result they are not happy, and they make hard work of serving God" (White, *Testimonies*, vol. 5, p. 278). These have not accepted the Spirit to live within them as an ever-present internal guide.

That does not mean that most of the members of the church were not once converted. But probably our condition today is like that of our church in 1901. At the General Conference session that year Ellen White said in one of her sermons: "The time has come when this people are to be born again. Those that have never been born again, and those that have forgotten that they were purged from their old sins, . . . would better be converted" (Ellen G. White, in *General Conference Bulletin*, 1901, p. 26).

One of the joys of spring and early summer for us is to plant a garden. So in the spring of 1989 we again planted a garden. It was bigger than usual, since we had moved to a new location and had more garden space available.

In early June the carrots, beets, squash, and cucumbers were just coming up when we had to go away. We stayed away for six weeks. We had a man care for the lawn, but there was no one to look after the garden. When we returned home we no longer had a garden. It was a jungle. The potatoes were fine, and even ready to dig and eat. The peppers and tomatoes we could still find, as well as pumpkin and squash vines. These were all growing in untended profusion. But most of the beets and just about all the carrots had died. The small spindly carrots especially had apparently been choked to death by the flourishing weeds and the cucumbers and squash that had invaded their area. When we left home and our garden, all our crops had been growing and doing well. But left to themselves, some had been unable to cope successfully with the prolific weeds and more vigorous garden growth.

Our garden is an apt picture of a person's spiritual life. A person may have been born again. He is alive in Christ. And he is growing in grace. But then he suddenly becomes too busy to tend his spiritual garden. It is neglected, like our garden. And before long the weeds of thinking and doing, not conducive to spiritual life and growth, crowd out his interest in God and His will.

In a world of sin, evil is more viable than good. After all, this is still Satan's kingdom, and the old carnal nature has squatter's rights within us. Even though Jesus bought it back at Calvary, He has not yet taken over management of this planet. He will not actively do so until after the millennium. So Satan is still running the farm, as it were, although it legally belongs to Jesus.

Under such conditions a person who wants to grow a soul for heavenly society and the new earth must constantly weed out many thoughts and interests that lead away from God and His will. He must do the same with activities and entertainments that tend to lead away from God-pleasing activities and recreation.

The apostle Paul's advice to us is: "If then you have been raised with Christ, seek the things that are above, where Christ is, seated at the right hand of God. Set your minds on things that are above, not on things that are on earth. For you have died, and your life is hid with Christ in God. When

Christ who is our life appears, then you also will appear with him in glory'' (Col. 3:1-4). "Finally, brethren, whatever is true, whatever is honorable, whatever is just, whatever is pure, whatever is lovely, whatever is gracious, if there is any excellence, if there is anything worthy of praise, think about these things'' (Phil. 4:8).

---

* "Heart" in the Bible refers but seldom to the literal body organ. The new heart (see Eze. 11:19; 18:31; 36:26) that God is willing and eager to give everyone refers to a person's changed attitude, desires, ambitions, and impelling motives.

C H A P T E R 12

VALLEY OF
DRY BONES

Based on Ezekiel 37

The vision of the valley of dry bones came to Ezekiel after the fall of Jerusalem. By that time Daniel and his companions had been in Babylon almost 20 years. Ezekiel and his fellow captives who arrived in Babylon with King Jehoiachin had been there about a dozen years, and the latest arrivals had just come. For this vision Ezekiel was taken by the Spirit from his home by the river Chebar to a valley covered with dry bones.

To all the captive Jews the situation appeared hopeless. Judah had ceased to exist as a nation. This had not been the case when the first two contingents of Jewish captives came to Babylon. On those occasions the nation had been spared and there was still hope. But not so at this time.

With the burning of Solomon's magnificent Temple, the razing of Jerusalem, and the total subjugation of their country, the last hope of the captives had vanished. They pictured themselves and their country as Ezekiel saw in his vision: a valley of dry bones. The disconsolate Jews were saying to one another: "Our bones are dried up, and our hope is lost; we are clean cut off" (Eze. 37:11).

These dry bones had once represented the God-favored nation ruled over by David and Solomon. As Ezekiel looked at these dry bones, the Lord asked him: "Son of man, can these bones live?" In utter hopelessness Ezekiel's only answer was: "O Lord God, thou knowest" (verse 3).

Then the Lord asked Ezekiel to preach to the dry bones. To the prophet this appeared simply ludicrous. For years he had preached to living people and the response had been insignificant. And now God told him to preach to these very dry bones. It did not make sense; it was hopeless. Nevertheless, he followed God's admonition, with the assurance that if he followed the counsel, God would put flesh on the dry bones and cause breath to come back into them. And as Ezekiel preached, a miracle happened. The bones, tinder-dry in the sun, began to move. Skeletons were reassembled. Then the skeletons were covered with sinews, flesh, and skin. But as yet, there was no life in them.

Then God again said to Ezekiel: "Prophesy to the breath, prophesy, son of man, and say to the breath, Thus says the Lord God: Come from the four winds, O breath, and breathe upon these slain, that they may live" (verse 9). As he did that, the dry bones "lived, and stood upon their feet, an exceedingly great host" (verse 10).

"Part of the artistry of this chapter is the skillful use of the Hebrew word *ruah*. This appears in three different translations; as Spirit in verses 1 and 14, as breath in verses 5, 6, 8, 9 and 10, and as wind or winds in verse 9. But in reality it is the same word every time, and no English translation can do justice to its variety of meaning. The Greek word, *pneuma*, shares the flexibility of the Hebrew, and LXX [the Septuagint, a Greek translation of the Old Testatment from the third century B.C.] was able to use it consistently in this passage. It is the same word that lies behind the double meaning of wind and Spirit in John 3:8. As its root *ruah* denotes the sense of 'air in motion,' i.e., wind or breath. This can extend from a gentle breeze to a raging passion. It comes to mean both man's spirit, or 'disposition' and also emotional qualities like vigor, courage, impatience, and ecstasy. It covers not only man's vital breath, given to him at birth and leaving his body in his dying gasp, but also the Spirit of God who imparts that breath. Such is the rich variety of the word used here by Ezekiel" (Taylor, *Ezekiel*, p. 237).

The basic point of the valley of dry bones is Israel's restoration as a nation. It was God's positive assurance that even though His people were spiritually dead in trespasses and sins, there would be a resurrection to new spiritual life with a subsequent restoration of them as a nation in Palestine.

Israel had nearly been obliterated by sin. Their spiritual death had made them succumb to sinful attitudes and habits. This in turn led to political weakness and ultimate extinction as an independent nation. If they had faithfully continued in their covenant relationship with God, they would never have become a broken reed of a nation subject to foreign powers. No Babylonian general would have captured Jerusalem and conquered Judah as a nation. No governor appointed by Babylon—like Gedaliah—would have ruled within its walls. The end of their national independence was but the result of their apostasy from God.

The captives in Babylon, after the fall of Jerusalem and Zedekiah's captivity, looked upon themselves as the inhabitants of the northern kingdom had done after their conquest by Assyria. They ruefully recognized that the bright promises made to their forefathers through Abraham, Moses, and David had come to naught. Though the captives were physically alive, courage and hope had vanished. They were as good as dead. And of course, by and by all as individuals would die physically.

But God was not intimidated. Even though neither the captives nor those left in Judah could espy any hope for the future, God did. He had a wonderful future in mind for all His scattered captives throughout the East. As He was able to resurrect the dry bones by His Spirit, so He was able to restore them as a nation. He envisioned a good future for all those who would respond to the wooings of His Spirit. By His Spirit they could all become new men and women.

The regeneration of the dry lifeless bones in the valley of death aptly symbolizes the spiritual renewal of the Jewish nation foreshadowed in Ezekiel 33-36. God's wish envisioned a nation tempered and spiritually wiser through the Babylonian captivity and gladly willing to choose His way rather than insisting on their own way. They had despised God's plan for them, and their own had brought them, not hoped-for national prosperity and personal happiness, but national captivity and untold personal grief.

These Jews, purified in the furnace of affliction, God would gather and assemble in their own country of Israel. And not only these, but also the Israelites scattered throughout the East. The original undivided people of Israel were to be restored as He had first planted them in Canaan.

There is no doubt that Ezekiel 37 speaks of spiritual revival rather than literal resurrection of the dead. But for a few moments we will consider the ultimate resurrection of the dead—the resurrection of true Israel from all the earth.

At the end of salvation history God will gather His spiritually born again, even those who were once virtually as dead to spiritual things as these dead bones were physically dead. The return of the Jews from Babylonian captivity and the scattered remnants of the Israelites in Assyrian captivity were but types of the great and final gathering from all nations of the redeemed at the very end of time.

The apostle Paul explains that the true Jews are not Jews according to the flesh, but are in reality those who are God's children by faith. They are those who in past times have been and today are loyal to His will.

Loyalty rests on trust. Those who trust God are His children, irrespective of what blood flows through their veins and pulsates through their bodies or from where they come. "For he is not a Jew, which is one outwardly; neither is that circumcision, which is outward in the flesh: but he is a Jew, which is one inwardly, and circumcision is that of the heart, in the spirit, and not in the letter; whose praise is not of men, but of God" (Rom. 2:28, 29, KJV).

Ezekiel himself repeatedly emphasizes the spiritual nature of God's elect. It is these that He will gather from all nations (see Eze. 11:17-19). Those who have responded to God's imperative that "ye must be born again" (John 3:7, KJV) and remained in that commitment will share eternity with Him.

Ezekiel's parable of the dry bones is not limited in its

application to ancient Israel. It applies to you and me as members of God's Israel today. Unfortunately, what was true anciently is still true of us as God's church today. "Many who are without spiritual life have their names on the church records, but they are not written in the Lamb's book of life. They may be joined to the church, but they are not united to the Lord" (*The SDA Bible Commentary*, Ellen G. White Comments, vol. 4, p. 1166).

Without the Holy Spirit no one is alive in Christ (see Rom. 8:9). Rather, we are like Ezekiel's valley of dry bones. Ellen White wrote: "Not only does this simile of the dry bones apply to the world, but also to those who have been blessed with great light; for they also are like the skeletons of the valley. They have the form of men, the framework of the body; but they have not spiritual life. But the parable does not leave the dry bones merely knit together into the forms of men; for it is not enough that there is symmetry of limb and feature. The breath of life must vivify the bodies, that they might stand upright, and spring into activity. These bones represent the house of Israel, the church of God, and the hope of the church is the vivifying influence of the Holy Spirit. The Lord must breathe upon the dry bones, that they may live" (*ibid.*, pp. 1165, 1166).

In the latter part of chapter 37 (verses 15-28), Ezekiel acted out another parable. He took two sticks and held them end to end in his hand. They looked like one. When the people saw this, they asked him what it meant.

Ezekiel answered that God would take the remains of the two kingdoms of Israel and Judah, represented respectively by Ephraim and Joseph, scattered throughout the East through the Assyrian and Babylonian captivities, and again make them into one nation.

To the distraught Jews living in Babylon this was another message of hope and joy. So hopeful that they hardly dared to think it. But Ezekiel had again fanned their flame of hope and helped keep their vision of a restored Israel alive in the hearts of the captives. In the remaining chapters of his book Ezekiel presents God's glorious plan for a restored Israel in greater detail.

When God established Israel as a nation and settled them in Canaan after the Exodus, it had never been His plan that they should be two nations. They were to be one prosperous and strong nation under His own leadership exercised through leaders like Moses and Joshua, or a good judge like Samuel, or kings like David and Solomon (in his early years). But through disobedience to God and departure from His ways and plan, the nation of Israel had separated into two nations.

The calamity of captivity for both Israel and Judah God would use as a means of fulfilling His plan of reuniting them into one nation. In this way God's purpose would again be fulfilled. For us as individuals this should be a constant source of encouragement. Even if we temporarily refuse to follow God's will He will not reject us permanently. He will try patiently to lead us to the destination He had in mind for us originally by way of a circuitous route. Literally He did that for Israel during the Exodus. Since they through murmuring and sinfulness refused to let God lead them along a direct route into Canaan, God devised a new plan along a meandering route over four decades instead of 40 days.

He will do the same in your life and mine. He will not give up on our salvation. He constantly devises new means to reach us with salvation as long as we live.

The valley of dry bones assures us of a physical resurrection. Many people live only for this world. They believe death ends everything. They therefore try to get all they possibly can out of this life by any means—fair or foul.

Such a philosophy of life becomes understandable in light of their assumption that death is the absolute end. But their assumption is erroneous. There is life beyond the grave. In God's plan earthly life is but a prelude to our real or eternal life. It was eternal life God had in mind for humans when He created Adam and Eve.

But the belief that there will be a real bodily resurrection has faded from the minds of many today. Some scoff at the idea. The Word of God, on the other hand, presents life beyond the tomb not as an empty dream but as a consoling reality. This divine reality removes the sting of death. It is in view of this that the apostle Paul triumphantly cries out, "O death, where is thy victory? O death, where is thy sting?" (1 Cor. 15:55).

The Christian hope of the resurrection and life beyond the grave turns the dreadfulness of death into a peaceful sleep.

Ezekiel's valley of dry bones presents the divine assurance of both a spiritual and a physical resurrection with life eternal in a land where God "will wipe away every tear" and "never again shall there be sorrow or crying or pain. For all those former things are past and gone" (Rev. 21:4, Phillips).

Jeremiah harbored the same invincible faith in the future of restored Israel that Ezekiel did. When Babylonian siege works could be seen outside the walls of Jerusalem and it was obvious that the enemy would soon be masters of the city, he bought a field at Anathoth, near Jerusalem, from his cousin Hanameel (see Jer. 32). He weighed out its purchase price, 17 shekels of silver, and signed the papers before witnesses.

To a person without faith in God, such a transaction was sheer stupidity. Business was at a standstill. Anathoth was already in the hands of the Babylonians, and soon the whole country would be theirs. The average person despaired of the future. Apart from faith in God and His Word this purchase was worthless. "This entire transaction demonstrates the tremendous faith which Jeremiah had in the divine promises of national renewal," R. K. Harrison aptly observes (*Jeremiah and Lamentations* [Downers Grove, Ill.: Inter-Varsity Press, 1973], p. 42).

Faith, or trust in God's promises, is good. But there are times that demand more than quiet confidence that God will fulfill His promises. That was the case when Jeremiah bought his cousin's parcel of land at his native Anathoth. The people both in and outside the city had relinquished all hope. Jeremiah's demonstration of faith was for the benefit of these despairing people. Jeremiah himself did not need any empirical evidence that the country would again be settled by returning exiles. He knew God, and he trusted His promise. But the people needed this demonstration of faith in order to believe. And so Jeremiah acted out his faith.

Jeremiah's action of buying this field against all reason inspired them with faith in God's promise. It instilled renewed hope in God's faithful ones within the city walls that this was not the end for either Jerusalem or Judah. They realized that "houses and fields and vineyards shall again be bought in this land" (Jer. 32:15).

Israel had failed. But God planned to give them another chance. He would spiritually resurrect them both as individuals and as a nation, even though they appeared as a valley of dry bones. He depended on them. Whether or not they were willing to receive the new heart, He was longing to give it to every one of them.

CHAPTER 13

GOD'S GLORIOUS POSTEXILIC PLAN FOR ISRAEL

● *Based on Ezekiel 38-48*

In the last 11 chapters of his book—chapters 38-48—Ezekiel presents a serendipitous picture of God's envisioned future for postexilic Israel. First He is going to free them from captivity. Then He is going to gather all who are willing as He would grains of wheat and replant them in their ancestral homeland. All these chapters picture a time of unparalleled security and personal peace for reunited and restored Israel living in the new covenant relationship with their God.

Chapters 38 and 39 present God as the all-caring guardian of His people Israel. No conqueror, military or otherwise, however powerful, would be able to harm them. They were to enjoy protection from all enemies even in a "land of unwalled villages" (Eze. 38:11), though enemies would come up against them (see verse 16).

About a half century later, after some of the captives had returned to their native land, the prophet Zechariah reiterated God's promise of security and peace for His people. Ezekiel gave his prophecy to instill hope in the despondent captives. Zechariah repeated God's pledge of protection and security to dispel despair among the struggling returnees, who amid difficulties were attempting to establish themselves and rebuild Jerusalem.

Zechariah told his fellows who were disheartened by Jerusalem's small population that one day the people of Jerusalem would be so numerous that no wall would suffice to contain them, "because of the multitude of men and cattle in it." Nor would a wall be needed, for God's promise to them was: "I will be to her [Jerusalem] a wall of fire round about, . . . and I will be the glory within her" (Zech. 2:4, 5).

As postexilic Israel would choose to live in the new covenant experience, God Himself would encamp among them and be "as a guard" around them (Zech. 9:8). And no oppressor would again overrun them. God would verily permit Gog and his cohorts to come up against Israel (Eze. 39:2), but God Himself would be Israel's defender both against Gog and any enemy. Gog and his armies would be utterly defeated and become food for birds and beasts of prey (verse 4).

Through Gog's total defeat in his attack on Israel the nations would learn that Israel's God is indeed "the Holy One in Israel" (verse 7) and mighty to save. In Israel's prior history God's name had often been profaned when Israel had met defeat before its enemies. By Israel's defeat the heathen had come to believe that Israel's God was like their gods, helpless and unable to protect them from danger (verse 7).

But this was to change. No longer would Israel need weapons to defend themselves against their enemies. They would therefore destroy their implements of war (see Eze. 39:9), as Gog and his multitude would meet their end with burial in the land of Israel (verses 11-16).

By virtue of Israel's prosperity under the new covenant experience they themselves and all nations would "know that the house of Israel went into captivity for their iniquity, because they dealt so treacherously with me [God] that I hid my face from them and gave them into the hand of their adversaries, and they all fell by the sword. I dealt with them according to their uncleanness and their transgressions, and hid my face from them" (verses 23, 24).

God's purpose for postexilic Israel was safety and security inside God's hedge. At the Exodus the Israelites had been immune to Balaam's curses on the plains of Moab prior to their entering the Promised Land. For monetary reward Balaam longed to curse Israel (see 2 Peter 2:15). But under divine inspiration he was prompted to say: "Behold, I have received a command to bless; He has blessed, and I cannot reverse it. He has not observed iniquity in Jacob, nor has He seen wickedness in Israel. The Lord his God is with him, and the shout of a King is among them. . . . For there is no sorcery against Jacob, nor is there any divination against Israel" (Num. 23:20-23, NKJV).

In the new covenant experience Israel would be as secure and prosperous as Job, inside God's hedge (see Job 1:10). No longer would He hide His face from them or be angry with them, but the Lord would make His face shine upon them and be gracious to them in fulfillment of the Aaronic benediction (see Num. 6:25), as they would choose to live under the guidance of the Holy Spirit (see Eze. 39:29), and do God's will.

Israel never saw the fulfillment of this prophetic panorama of God's complete physical protection from other nations. They failed to meet His condition of total commitment to Him and His will. But these promises and plans for a restored Israel will meet complete fulfillment in the concluding phase of the great controversy. Satan at the head of rebels against God from all ages, under the names of Gog and Magog, will then be defeated, while the redeemed under the leadership of Jesus will be safe from his onslaughts inside the Holy City. Satan and his hosts will be destroyed and blotted out from both the earth and the universe (see Rev. 20:7-10). After that the redeemed will live on this earth *made new* by cleansing fire in the very presence of God for eternity.

Chapters 40-48 are Ezekiel's last prophecy. They continue to unravel God's plan for His people in connection with their God-envisioned postexilic temple. This prophecy would have become reality if His professed people had faithfully fulfilled God's purpose for them. But the majority of the exiles and their descendants never returned. Most of them remained in the countries to which they had originally been taken as captives, or to which they had chosen to flee.

The Jewish historian Abram Sachar says about his people after the fall of Jerusalem in 586 B.C.: "A remnant of the population lived on in Palestine, another was carried off to Babylon, a third fled to Egypt" (*A History of the Jews* [New York: Alfred Knopf, 1964], p. 78). Ezekiel's contemporary portrait was: "My sheep were scattered over all the face of the earth, with none to search or seek for them" (Eze. 34:6).

Into Egypt Jews had dribbled for centuries. Even before the destruction of Jerusalem, flourishing Jewish communities existed in many parts of Pharaoh's dominions. During the sixth century B.C. their numbers grew. After the murder of the Babylonian-appointed governor Gedaliah at Mizpah (see Jer. 41:2), a large number of Jews fled to Egypt against the eagerly sought advice of Jeremiah (Jer. 42:1-14). In doing so, they took Jeremiah with them (see Jer. 43:5-7). Others drifted to other countries.

In Egypt Jews were prominent in helping build the wealth and strength of the Elephantine region. Some centuries later the Egyptian communities became leading commercial and cultural centers in the Jewish world.

The fewest Jews lived in Babylon. But they were the wealthiest, most cultured, and morally best Jews, since only such had been taken into Babylonian captivity (see Jer. 24:1-9). At first they lived together in almost autonomous colonies and tried to continue the life they had lived in Palestine, while they wept and hung their harps on the willow trees as they remembered Zion (see Ps. 137:1, 2). But they soon adjusted their thinking to their captivity and prayed for Babylon's welfare, as Jeremiah had counseled them (see Jer. 29:4-7).

It was impossible for these rustic, provincial Hebrews not to be affected by the splendors of this new civilization. Transplanted, as they were, from their Judean hinterlands to the center of power and to the heart of the Mesopotamian garden lands, they, like their kinsmen in Egypt, soon left farming. They became successful artisans, traders, and merchants. Ezekiel called Babylon "a land of trade" with cities "of merchants" (Eze. 17:4).

The exiled Jews adapted to this rich and powerful country teeming with life, and turned to trade and commerce. They rose on the wings of their shrewdness and soon became an influential group in the land of their forced adoption. "It was during the Babylonian and the Greek periods that the Jews in the Dispersion began to lay the foundation for the 'Golden Internationalism,' that is, Jewish control of the world's money" (Lars P. Qualben, *A History of the Christian Church* [New York: Thomas Nelson and Sons, 1942], p. 23). Their association with the past soon snapped as they quickly became part and parcel of Babylonian life.

By the end of the prophesied 70 years of captivity most of them were unwilling to forsake their luxuriously comfortable homes and lucrative businesses and return to their own backward country. To them emancipation did not mean freedom, but a return to financial restrictions or virtual bondage. So only a fraction of the exiles returned. Jerusalem never became overcrowded with people as the prophet Zechariah had envisioned (see Zech. 2:4).

God's plan of gathering all the Israelites, both the descendants of the northern tribes taken into Assyrian captivity and those taken into Babylonian captivity, to their ancestral homeland in Palestine never materialized.

The majority of them chose to remain in the Diaspora. They were found everywhere, so that by the beginning of the Christian Era the Greek geographer Strabo could write: "They have penetrated already into every state, so that it is difficult to find a single place in the world in which their tribe has not been received and become dominant!" (in Sachar, *A History of the Jews*, p. 78).

Jews were strategically located everywhere in the then-known world. If they had been true witnesses for God, they could have effectively heralded and prepared the world for the first coming of Jesus. At the Council of Jerusalem about A.D. 49 the apostle James recognized their universal presence by saying that "Moses has been preached in every city from the earliest times and is read in the synagogues on every Sabbath" (Acts 15:21, NIV).

In the restored kingdom of Israel racial exclusiveness would no longer exist. As the returnees occupied and redivided the land among the 12 original tribes (see Eze. 47:13), the strangers who joined the Israelites were to inherit land with the ethnic Israelites. God Himself directed: "They shall be to you as native-born sons of Israel" (verse 22).

"Heaven's plan of salvation is broad enough to embrace the whole world. . . . And He will not permit any soul to be disappointed who is sincere in his longing for something higher and nobler than anything the world can offer" (White, *Prophets and Kings*, pp. 377, 378).

"It was God's purpose that the strangers should be drawn to Israel, settle among them, and accept the religion of the true God" *(The SDA Bible Commentary*, vol. 4, p. 737). But neither God's plans with reference to the gathering of Israel nor the settlement of strangers among them as part of Israel ever met fulfillment.

Nevertheless, Ezekiel, not foreseeing its nonfulfillment, must have thrilled with joy to receive this vision of Israel's future in his homeland. With sorrow he had been compelled to announce God's withdrawal from His people because of their moral corruption and persistent rebellion. But now it was his privilege to announce their restoration as God's chosen people, as they would choose to live in the new covenant experience. What an exhilarating joy for Ezekiel to receive the prophecy that in Israel's future, Jerusalem would be known among the surrounding nations as "The Lord is there" (Eze. 48:35).

In order to enable the people to live in accordance with God's will, the priests were to impart knowledge to them. They were to teach the "people the difference between the holy and the common, and show them how to distinguish between the unclean and the clean" (Eze. 44:23). In the past they had been "destroyed for lack of knowledge" (Hosea 4:6).

Human nature dictates that knowledge that is not used or at least rehearsed in memory will gradually fade away and be lost. To guard against this, Moses admonished: "And these words which I command you this day shall be upon your heart; and you shall teach them diligently to your children, and shall talk of them when you sit in your house, and when you walk by the way, and when you lie down, and when you rise. And you shall bind them as a sign upon your hand, and they shall be as frontlets between your eyes. And you shall write them on the doorposts of your house and on your gates" (Deut. 6:6-9).

Joshua's advice was the same. He said: "This book of the law shall not depart out of your mouth, but you shall meditate on it day and night, that you may be careful to do according to all that is written on it; for then you shall make your way prosperous, and then you shall have good success" (Joshua 1:8). The revivals in Judah during the reigns of Hezekiah and Josiah had both resulted from a renewed interest in and devotion to the Word of God.

The ideal of systematic teaching of the Word of God amid the unsettled conditions and troublous times of the returning exiles was difficult or well-nigh impossible to maintain. The books of Ezra and Nehemiah show some sketches of postexilic history. But both unveil forgetfulness and apostasy from God's law. Ezra bemoaned mixed marriages. Both also depict heroic attempts to restore the knowledge and practice of the law of Moses among the people. To that end Ezra and the Levites read the law of Moses clearly to the people in preparation for and during one Feast of Tabernacles (see Neh. 8:2, 3, 8, 13-18). But these incidents were probably like single logs floating down a river.

The book of Malachi, possibly written during the time of Nehemiah or shortly after, mirrors the spiritual declension. "To be sure, the exiles had returned from the land of their captivity to the Land of Promise, but in their hearts they remained in the far country of disobedience and forgetfulness of God. . . . Eight times the Lord addresses the people and their religious leaders, graciously and patiently calling attention to one aspect after another of their apostasy, and eight times they petulantly deny any degree of imperfection (Mal. 1:2, 6, 7; 2:13, 14, 17; 3:7, 8, 13, 14)" *(The SDA Bible Commentary,* vol. 4, pp. 1121, 1122). The people in postexilic

Israel enjoyed a conceited sense of Laodicean self-satisfaction with their spiritual experience, life, and doings.

Ezekiel's prophecies in chapters 38-48 were conditional. They present God's plan for a born-again postexilic Israel. But they were never fulfilled, because not even restored Israel chose to abide by God's covenant with them by clinging to Him and His will rather than to their sins.

The captivity verily cured the Israelites of their worship of idols in the form of graven images. In captivity they became convinced that their prosperity depended upon their "obedience to the law of God. But with many of the people, obedience was not the outflow of faith and love. Their motives were selfish. Outward service was rendered as a means of attaining to national greatness" (White, *Prophets and Kings*, p. 708).

But that did not mean that it effectively cured them of the essence of idolatry. The essence of idolatry is to give priority in one's thoughts and affections to something besides God. Paul told the Colossian believers that even covetousness is idolatry (see Col. 3:5).

God had good plans for restored Israel. But the fulfillment of these promises of peace and security with material prosperity and a coveted standing among the nations rested on their faithful covenant relationship with Him. Instead of a curse, Israel was to be a blessing among the nations (Zech. 8:13; cf. Isa. 60:15). Through postexilic Israel God purposed to fulfill the promise He gave to Abraham that "thou shalt be a blessing" (Gen. 12:2).

"These promises were conditional on obedience. The sins that had characterized the Israelites prior to the captivity were not to be repeated. 'Execute true judgment,' the Lord exhorted those who were engaged in rebuilding; 'and show mercy and compassions every man to his brother: and oppress not the widow, nor the fatherless, the stranger, nor the poor; and let none of you imagine evil against his brother.' 'Speak ye every man the truth to his neighbor; execute the judgment of truth and peace in your gates' (Zech. 7:9, 10; 8:16)" *(ibid.,* p. 704).

It is both interesting and vitally important to notice that

God was not merely asking for mechanical or outward compliance with His will. He envisioned their doing His will from a heart directed by the Holy Spirit. Their thoughts were to run in the channels of God's will. Their religion would no longer consist of mere conformity—instead, it would spring from genuine conversion to God's plan. On that basis the future of the returning exiles was as bright as the promises of God.

But the Israelites failed to capitalize on God's plan for them. The Babylonian captivity did not cure them of idolatry. It became just as rampant among postexilic Israel as it had been before their captivity. It only became more subtle and not so easily discernible as their earlier worship of idols in the form of graven images.

Because the Israelites failed to cooperate, God's good plans for Israel were never fulfilled. "They would have met a literal fulfillment in the centuries following had Israel fully accepted God's purposes concerning them. The failure of Israel made impossible the fulfillment of these prophecies in their original intent" *(The SDA Bible Commentary,* vol. 4, p. 703).

These words of the poet John Greenleaf Whittier certainly apply to God's postexilic Israel:

"For of all sad words of tongue and pen,
The saddest are these: 'It might have been!' "

But for every Spirit-born Christian who chooses to live in the new covenant relationship with God, an even better future beckons in God's eternal kingdom.

SCRIPTURAL INDEX

(exclusive of Ezekiel)

BIBLE BOOKSHELF
These mini-commentaries will bring a richer blessing to your Bible study.

Blessed Assurance, by William G. Johnsson. Habakkuk and Hebrews both speak to Christians today in a manner that is often startling. Paper, 144 pages. US$6.95, Cdn$8.70.

The God Who Says Yes, by Walter Scragg. In the book of Luke we see a God and a Saviour who accepted everybody, including publicans, women, and others whom society looked down on. Paper, 128 pages. US$6.95, Cdn$8.70.

God's Church in a Hostile World, by Joseph J. Battistone. The author draws on Old Testament passages to help us understand John's visions as recorded in the book of Revelation. Paper, 140 pages. US$7.95, Cdn$9.95.

God's Solution to Man's Dilemma, by Herbert Kiesler. The author explores the theme of righteousness by faith, which undergirds the book of Romans. Paper, 128 pages. US$7.95, Cdn$9.95.

The In-between God, by Walter Scragg. In this study on Acts, the Holy Spirit is portrayed as the "In-between God," the one who mediates, enables, and persuades. Paper, 128 pages. US$6.95, Cdn$8.70.

In the Beginning, by Arthur J. Ferch. The author explores the themes of Genesis and provides spiritual insights into this fascinating book of beginnings. Paper, 141 pages. US$6.95, Cdn$8.70.

Let Daniel Speak, by G. Arthur Keough. Get a clearer view of a God who is active in history, who does not leave us alone to fend for ourselves. Paper, 128 pages. US$6.95, Cdn$8.70.

Love Come Home, by Robert H. Pierson. Using the books Hosea and Philemon, the author explores how God's people should respond to His great love for them today. Paper, 125 pages. US$6.95, Cdn$8.70.

Never Far From Grace, by Rosalie Haffner Lee. The books of 1 and 2 Samuel present God's people making choices that will shape their destiny. But no matter how poor the decision, they are never far from God's grace. Paper, 128 pages. US$7.95, Cdn$9.95.

Portraits of the Messiah in Zechariah, by Philip G. Samaan. Each chapter focuses on a different aspect of Christ's character and ministry. Paper, 128 pages. US$7.95, Cdn$9.95.

Available at your Adventist Book Center, or write to: ABC Mailing Service, P.O. Box 1119, Hagerstown, MD 21741.

Send check or money order. Enclose applicable sales tax and 15 percent (minimum US$2.50) for postage and handling. Prices and availability subject to change without notice.